Tastes
from a
Tuscan Kitchen

THE HIPPOCRENE COOKBOOK LIBRARY

Tastes
from a
Tuscan Kitchen

MADELINE ARMILLOTTA

~ & ~

DIANE NOCENTINI

HIPPOCRENE BOOKS, INC.
New York

Illustrations by Madeline Armillotta
Book design adapted from a design by Michael Yee

For more information, address:
HIPPOCRENE BOOKS, INC.
171 Madison Avenue
New York, NY 10016
www.hippocrenebooks.com

ISBN-13: 978-0-7818-1147-7
ISBN-10: 0-7818-1147-3

Cataloging-in-Publication Data available from the Library of Congress.

Printed in the United States of America.

Our most heartfelt thanks to
Ermanno Carnieri, Alessandro Senatori and Massimo Benozzi
for their computer wizardry and kind assistance.

We would be amiss if we did not thank our editor,
Barbara Keane-Pigeon, for her professional
and unfailing assistance.

For
Mimmo and Vicky
&
Paolo, Sam, and Elena
with
gratitude and love.

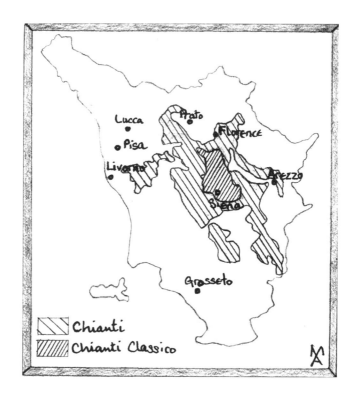

Lucca
Prato
Pisa
Florence
Livorno
Arezzo
Siena
Grosseto

Chianti
Chianti Classico

Tuscany

Introduzione
INTRODUCTION

To be always talking about food is inevitable when living in Italy: just as the English talk about the weather or their gardens, so the Italians constantly share culinary delights. The cultural differences that exist between the two countries are evident when it comes to food, as the English "eat to live" and the Italians "live to eat." Whether you like it or not, in Tuscany cooking becomes a very central part of your life, especially with the absence of "ready meals" in Italian supermarkets.

A healthy Mediterranean diet is based on fresh fruit, vegetables, fish, meat, dairy products, pasta, beans, and olive oil. Combined with eating only three meals a day (without snacking on unhealthy, high-calorie foods) this diet can only lead to a healthy lifestyle.

We are two friends, English and Canadian, who happen to live in the same small village of Incisa, approximately $15^{1}/_{2}$ miles outside of Florence. When we read in recipes such lines as "marinade the venison" or "flambé the sauce," and so on, our hearts sink, as we know that we have neither the time nor the inclination to cook these sorts of dishes. Those are the kinds of cookbooks that are instantly relegated to gather dust to the living room bookcase. We have aimed to create an easy-to-prepare, family-oriented cookbook, based on wholesome Tuscan recipes. We would like to share with you all of our favorite dishes.

As we live in Tuscany, the recipes here are very much influenced by local dishes and traditions and, in a way, are also very personal. The last thing we wanted to do was write the "classical" Italian or Tuscan cookbook. Rather we wished to share with you our experiences of everyday cooking and the dishes that we've found most popular. We have included many ideas from women who live in the quaint mountain villages of Tuscany, and also some from neighboring areas; Madeline's husband and family come from the southern region of Puglia. Some influences of the "cucina povera" (peasant style cooking) are also apparent, as are some northern recipes we received from enthusiastic friends living in this region.

We have only included recipes that we think are suitable for English and North American taste buds, so anything to do with offal, brains, and pig's feet has been avoided. There are also many recipes for vegetarians and some for children who are reluctant eaters.

We hope that this book will be an inspiration not just for Italian-style cooking but also for general meal planning, especially when one is confronted with the usual dilemma of "What am I going to cook today?" We believe that it will become a well-thumbed friend and stay in a handy kitchen drawer, supplying a constant source of ideas for day-to-day cooking with many "Tastes from a Tuscan Kitchen" thrown in for good measure.

Happy Cooking and Buon Appetito!

Sommario

CONTENTS

Consigli Da Una Dispensa Italiana
TIPS FROM AN ITALIAN PANTRY

EXTRA-VIRGIN OLIVE OIL

Olive oil is the most essential ingredient in Italian cooking. This oil is quite irre-placeable in any dish and, therefore, it is of vital importance to buy only the best extra-virgin cold-pressed variety. This variety has a rich green color and, when freshly pressed, it has a slightly piquant flavor. Good quality olive oil has high amounts of vitamin E and benefits good blood circulation. It has been doc-umented that people on a Mediterranean diet suffer less from heart disease, and we believe this should be taken into consideration the next time you have a choice of cooking with olive oil or butter.

FRESH HERBS

We strongly recommend growing your own herbs in a pot on a sunny window-sill or buying fresh herbs from your supermarket. Fresh herbs add a unique flavor to your cooking; after having compared fresh to dry, you too will be convinced. Most frequently used in Tuscan cooking are rosemary, sage, basil, and flat-leafed parsley. Rosemary and sage grow more or less all year round. Basil and parsley can be grown in abundance from May/June to September/October. We also suggest freezing fresh herbs. This way fresh-tasting herbs are always available, even through the winter. Just wash, dry, and freeze them in indi-vidual bags.

FRUIT AND NUTS

In Italy a vast selection of fruit is available. It is of high quality and Italians prefer to eat it when in season. In Tuscany, such desserts as fruit salad, straw-berries, peaches and cream, apple cake, lemon sorbet, and fruit-flavored gela-

to are all served in season. Pears are traditionally served with Gorgonzola or Pecorino cheese, and they are divine. Dried figs stuffed with walnuts are another tasty combination. Chestnuts, walnuts, pine nuts, hazelnuts, and almonds are the most popular nuts used in cooking, baking, and with salads. Chestnuts and walnuts are wonderful to use in turkey stuffing; toasted pine nuts and walnuts go well in salads, pesto, with various vegetables, and in some desserts; hazelnuts and almonds are used principally in desserts.

MUSHROOMS

Mushrooms (funghi) are an important constituent of Italian cuisine. Where mushrooms appear in our recipes, the cultivated button variety may be used; however, if fresh porcini mushrooms are available, you must try them—but the flavor of the dish will be altered. Dried porcini are sold in delicatessens and should be used sparingly, as they are rich in flavor. Fill a small saucepan to the three-quarter mark and add 2 cups of dried mushrooms. Simmer for 30 minutes. Remove the mushrooms with a slotted spoon. Through a strainer lined with paper towel, filter the water they have cooked in. The broth may be used in our Chicken Breasts with Onions recipe (pages 67–68, variation 2) and the mushrooms may be used in various dishes. In Tuscany, during the fall, porcini mushrooms feature in almost every course and are a delicacy that Italians truly enjoy.

PARMESAN CHEESE

This cheese is made in several towns and villages around Emilia-Romagna and originates from the city of Parma. It is yellow and grainy in texture, and has been aged from one to four years. We strongly recommend that you buy this cheese fresh and grate it as needed over pasta and rice dishes. Do not buy the grated Parmesan cheese in the small round containers that are so often sold in England and North America. It smells of old socks and bears no resemblance to the wonderful flavor of real parmigiano. Fresh Parmesan cheese is a rich source of calcium and is particularly beneficial to growing children and the elderly. When you are left with a Parmesan rind, a great way to make use of it is by adding it to soup. Parmesan rind adds a savory cheese flavor to all creamy soups.

PRESSURE COOKERS

We used to have an ingrained fear of pressure cookers. We regarded them as some kind of lethal time bomb. As pressure cookers are commonly used in Italy, we eventually coaxed ourselves into trying them and gradually overcame our fears, realizing what wonderful inventions they really are. We now use them almost daily for all vegetables, all dried beans, and some meat dishes. They are great timesavers and food retains all of its nutritional value, as nothing boils away. We have added the cooking times for using a pressure cooker in any relevant dishes.

RED HOT CHILE OIL

Red hot chile oil is used mainly in winter in soups and some pasta dishes. Once the soup is served in a bowl, just two or three drops (literally) are added to produce a hot effect. It can be added to minestrone, spelt, or barley soup and also pasta dishes, such as pasta and beans, pasta and chickpeas, or pasta and lentils.

> To make the oil:
> 1) Evenly chop 2 to 3 handfuls of dried red chile peppers.
> 2) Add the chiles to about 1 quart of olive oil. In time, the oil
>   will become red in color and red hot, too.

Don't forget to use it very sparingly, otherwise the food will be inedible, or even worse, your tongue may catch fire!

SALT

Salt is used much more in Italian cooking than in North American, and it can be tasted clearly in the prepared food. For example, pasta water is salted, as is the water in which vegetables are cooked. Since living in Italy, we have become accustomed to using more salt than we would have done in either England or Canada. But we will leave how much salt you use to your own personal taste and discretion.

TUSCAN BREAD

Every region in Italy has its own type of bread. The bread found in Tuscany has a crisp crust and is soft and spongy within. Tuscan bread is very different from any bread found elsewhere, as it is always baked in a wood oven, and is not baked in a loaf tin. In the old days, it was traditionally put into soups. It was also soaked down and squeezed out, then used in a variety of dishes, such as meatballs and salads. Tuscans have never been known to throw away bread and this tradition has remained, making bread an indispensable part of Tuscan cuisine. We recommend buying the most rustic type of artisan loaf available for serving with our dishes. However, we have not included any recipes requiring Tuscan bread as an ingredient. After many experiments using non-Tuscan bread in the same recipes, we came to the conclusion that the texture was not at all similar and the flavor of the dish was completely different.

Crostini

APPETIZERS

In Tuscany, crostini are traditional appetizers. They are light, versatile, easy to make, and are a wonderful finger food to share with company. We have chosen our favorites, as they represent the simplicity of Tuscan cuisine. Their distinct rich flavors offer a savory start to any meal.

Another typical Tuscan appetizer is a platter of fine-quality sliced meats, such as prosciutto crudo, salame Toscano, finocchiona, bresaola, and capocollo. These are served alongside a freshly sliced loaf and/or with a variety of crostini. Prosciutto crudo is also very popular and deliciously balanced when accompanied with sliced canteloupe or figs. Once again, delicate, simple flavors are prevalent.

The following recipes are based on serving four crostini per person. Also, we have calculated that the average baguette (loaf of French bread) provides twenty-four bread rounds, and our recipes have adequate ingredients for making this amount.

Crostini di Carciofi
ARTICHOKE CROSTINI

6 servings – preparation 15 min.

2 CLOVES GARLIC, FINELY CHOPPED
2 (8-OUNCE) CANS ARTICHOKE HEARTS, DRAINED AND COARSELY
  CHOPPED
1 (8-OUNCE) PACKAGE CREAM CHEESE
½ CUP GRATED PARMESAN CHEESE
1 BAGUETTE, SLICED INTO ROUNDS AND TOASTED

Combine the garlic and artichoke hearts in a bowl. Add the cream cheese and Parmesan. Mix well. If you prefer a smoother consistency, use an electric mixer until well-blended. Spread on toasted bread rounds and serve.

VARIATION:
This dish is also tasty served as a dip alongside toasted pita bread. Cut the pita bread into wedges and lay them on a baking pan. Bake at 350°F for 10 minutes.

Crostini ai Fagioli
CANNELLINI BEAN CROSTINI

6 servings – preparation 15 min. – cooking time 15 min.

---

2 TABLESPOONS OLIVE OIL, PLUS ADDITIONAL FOR DRIZZLING
3 CLOVES GARLIC, CRUSHED
3 LEAVES FRESH SAGE, FINELY CHOPPED
1 (14-OUNCE) CAN CANNELLINI BEANS, DRAINED
SALT AND BLACK PEPPER
1 BAGUETTE, SLICED INTO ROUNDS AND TOASTED

Heat the olive oil in a large nonstick skillet, and gently sauté the garlic and sage. Remove the garlic from the pan. Add the beans, a ¼ cup of water, and stir well. Simmer for about 10 minutes. Add salt and pepper to taste. Spoon the beans onto the toasted bread rounds, drizzle with olive oil, and serve.

Crostini al Salmone
SMOKED SALMON CROSTINI

6 servings – preparation 10 min.

---

1 (5-OUNCE) PACKAGE SMOKED SALMON
8 OUNCES CREAM CHEESE
1 TABLESPOON RED ONION, FINELY CHOPPED
1 TABLESPOON CHOPPED FRESH PARSLEY
½ TEASPOON GARLIC, FINELY CHOPPED
1 TEASPOON FRESHLY SQUEEZED LEMON JUICE
1 BAGUETTE, SLICED INTO ROUNDS AND TOASTED

In a food processor or blender, process all the ingredients except the bread to the desired consistency. Spread on the toasted bread rounds and serve.

Crostini con Pollo e Cipolla

CHICKEN AND ONION CROSTINI

6 servings – preparation 10 min. – cooking time 10 min.

2 TABLESPOONS EXTRA-VIRGIN OLIVE OIL
1 BONELESS CHICKEN BREAST
1 CUP MAYONNAISE
1 (4-OUNCE) JAR PICKLED ONIONS, DRAINED AND FINELY CHOPPED
SALT
1 BAGUETTE, SLICED INTO ROUNDS AND TOASTED

Heat the olive oil in a skillet over medium heat and sauté the chicken for about 10 minutes, until lightly browned. Let cool. Finely chop the cooled chicken and blend with the mayonnaise and onions. Add salt to taste. Spread on toasted rounds and serve.

Crostini con Melanzane

EGGPLANT CROSTINI

6 servings – preparation 10 min. – cooking time 30 min.

¼ CUP EXTRA-VIRGIN OLIVE OIL
3 TABLESPOONS FINELY CHOPPED FRESH PARSLEY
3 CLOVES GARLIC, CHOPPED
1 LARGE EGGPLANT, DICED
1 (8-OUNCE) CAN PLUM TOMATOES
SALT
1 BAGUETTE, SLICED INTO ROUNDS AND TOASTED

Heat the oil in a large lidded saucepan and sauté the parsley and garlic for two minutes. Add the eggplant and cook until soft. Add the canned tomatoes with juice and mash roughly. Add salt to taste. Cover and simmer for 30 minutes. Uncover and reduce the vegetables to a thick sauce. Spread the mixture on the bread rounds and serve.

Crostini coi Funghi
MUSHROOM CROSTINI

6 servings – preparation 15 min. – cooking time 15 min.

3 TABLESPOONS EXTRA-VIRGIN OLIVE OIL
3 CLOVES GARLIC, CHOPPED
1 POUND (ABOUT 3 CUPS) FRESH PORCINI OR BUTTON MUSHROOMS,
   FINELY CHOPPED
SALT
1 BAGUETTE, SLICED INTO ROUNDS AND TOASTED
3 TABLESPOONS CHOPPED FRESH PARSLEY

Heat the olive oil in a nonstick skillet and gently sauté the garlic. Add the mushrooms to the pan. Sauté over low heat for 15 minutes until the mushrooms are soft, and add salt to taste. Spoon the mushroom mixture onto the toasted bread rounds. Sprinkle with parsley and serve.

Crostini alla Cipolla
ONION CROSTINI

6 servings – preparation 10 min. – cooking time 15 min.

1 TABLESPOON EXTRA-VIRGIN OLIVE OIL
3 ONIONS, FINELY SLICED
1 TEASPOON SALT
DRIED OREGANO
1 BAGUETTE, SLICED INTO ROUNDS AND TOASTED

Heat the olive oil in a nonstick skillet and gently sauté the onions. Add the salt and a sprinkling of oregano. Cover and simmer over low heat for 15 minutes. Spoon onto the toasted bread rounds and serve.

Crostini al Pesto

PESTO CROSTINI

6 servings – preparation 20 min.

½ CUP PINE NUTS
⅔ CUP CHOPPED FRESH BASIL
4 WALNUTS
1 CLOVE GARLIC
¾ CUP EXTRA-VIRGIN OLIVE OIL
¼ CUP GRATED PARMESAN CHEESE
1 BAGUETTE, SLICED INTO ROUNDS AND TOASTED

In a food processor or blender, process ⅜ cup (¼ cup, plus half of a ¼-cup measure) of the pine nuts plus the basil, walnuts, garlic, oil, and Parmesan until smooth. By hand, gently mix in the remaining whole pine nuts. Spread on the toasted bread rounds and serve.

Crostini al Pomodoro

TOMATO AND HERB CROSTINI

6 servings – preparation 15 min.

This is one of our favorites. It's a simple recipe, yet truly delicious.

8 TO 10 RIPE PLUM TOMATOES, CHOPPED
3 CLOVES GARLIC, CHOPPED
3 TABLESPOONS CHOPPED FRESH BASIL
3 TABLESPOONS EXTRA-VIRGIN OLIVE OIL
1 TABLESPOON DRIED OREGANO
1 TABLESPOON SALT (OR TO TASTE)
1 TEASPOON BLACK PEPPER (OR TO TASTE)
1 BAGUETTE, SLICED INTO ROUNDS AND TOASTED

Combine all the ingredients except the bread, and mix well. Spoon onto the toasted bread rounds and serve.

Crostini ai Peperoni
RED AND YELLOW BELL PEPPER CROSTINI

6 servings – preparation 10 min. – cooking time 20 min.

---

2 TABLESPOONS EXTRA-VIRGIN OLIVE OIL
2 YELLOW BELL PEPPERS, SEEDED AND FINELY SLICED LENGTHWISE
2 RED BELL PEPPERS, SEEDED AND FINELY SLICED LENGTHWISE
4 CLOVES GARLIC, CHOPPED
SALT
1 BAGUETTE, SLICED INTO ROUNDS AND TOASTED

Heat the olive oil in a nonstick lidded skillet over medium heat. Add the peppers and ½ cup of water, stir, and cover the pan. Cook for 10 minutes. Add the garlic and the salt to taste, and cook, uncovered, until the peppers are soft and the water has reduced. Spoon onto the toasted bread rounds and serve.

Crostini con Salsiccia e Stracchino
ITALIAN GARLIC SAUSAGE AND STRACCHINO CHEESE CROSTINI

6 servings – preparation 20 min. – cooking time 5 min.

---

4 (½-POUND) ITALIAN GARLIC SAUSAGES
1 (8-OUNCE) PACKAGE STRACCHINO CREAM CHEESE
1 BAGUETTE, SLICED INTO ROUNDS AND TOASTED

Preheat broiler. Remove the casings from the sausages. Heat a skillet and crumble the sausage meat into it. Brown well. Drain the cooked sausage of its excess fat. Combine the sausage and cheese, and spread on the toasted bread rounds. Place under the broiler until golden.

VARIATION:
Cubed mozzarella cheese can be used instead of Stracchino.

Crostini di Tonno Grigliati

TUNA CROSTINI

6 servings – preparation 15 min. – cooking time 10 min.

2 TABLESPOONS OLIVE OIL
2 CARROTS, PEELED AND GRATED
1 ONION, CHOPPED
SALT
1 (10-OUNCE) CAN TUNA PACKED IN OLIVE OIL, DRAINED
3 TABLESPOONS CAPERS, DRAINED
2 TEASPOONS DRIED OREGANO
1 (8-OUNCE) PACKAGE BEL PAESE CHEESE, SLICED
1 BAGUETTE, SLICED INTO ROUNDS AND TOASTED

Preheat the broiler. Heat the olive oil in a small nonstick skillet and sauté the carrots and onion for 5 minutes until soft. Sprinkle with salt. In a mixing bowl, combine the tuna and capers. Add the cooked vegetables and the oregano. Mix well. Spread the tuna mixture on the toasted bread rounds and lay a slice of cheese on each. Broil until the cheese has melted. Serve immediately.

Crostini con Tonno e Capperi

TUNA AND CAPERS CROSTINI

6 servings – preparation 15 min.

1 (10-OUNCE) CAN TUNA PACKED IN OLIVE OIL, DRAINED
1 CUP MAYONNAISE
2 TABLESPOONS CAPERS, FINELY CHOPPED
SALT
1 BAGUETTE, SLICED INTO ROUNDS AND TOASTED

Mix the tuna with the mayonnaise. Add the capers to the tuna mixture. Add salt to taste. Spread on the toasted rounds of bread and serve.

Pizzette

MINI PIZZAS

6 servings – preparation 20 min. – cooking time 5 min.

---

4 TABLESPOONS ANCHOVY PASTE OR 8 ANCHOVY FILLETS,
   MASHED
⅔ CUP BUTTER
1 BAGUETTE, SLICED INTO ROUNDS AND TOASTED
1 (8-OUNCE) CAN TOMATO SAUCE
1 (8-OUNCE) PACKAGE MOZZARELLA, SLICED
CAPERS
DRIED OREGANO

Preheat the broiler. Mix the anchovy paste with the butter. Spread the mixture on the toasted bread rounds. Add to each round a layer of tomato sauce and a slice of mozzarella. Place a caper on top and sprinkle with oregano. Broil until the mozzarella starts to melt and turns slightly golden.

VARIATION:
There are many possible variations: replace the anchovy paste and butter mixture with sliced ham, olives, sausage, or sautéed onions.

Minestre e Insalate
SOUPS AND SALADS

*Soup appeases your hunger, quenches your thirst, fills your stomach,
aids the digestion, and puts color in your cheeks.*

—AN OLD ITALIAN SAYING

*With our frenetic lifestyles, it is all too easy to come home and open a can
of soup for supper. On the other hand, homemade soups are inexpensive
and, as most people have a pressure cooker and blender, easy to make.
Large quantities can be made and portions frozen for future meals. They
also constitute a wholesome and satisfying meal when served with a crusty
loaf of bread.*

Brodo di Carne

MEAT BROTH

12 servings – prep. 15 min. – cooking time 2 hr. (pressure cooker 30 min.)

---

2 CARROTS, PEELED
3 BOILING POTATOES, PEELED
1 ONION, PEELED
1 STALK CELERY
3 BAY LEAVES
1 TABLESPOON CHOPPED FRESH PARSLEY
3 PLUM TOMATOES, FRESH OR CANNED
2 POUNDS BEEF RIBS
1 TABLESPOON SALT (OR TO TASTE)

Fill a large saucepan with 3 quarts of water and bring to a boil. Add the carrots, potatoes, and onion to the pot, along with the celery, bay leaves, parsley, tomatoes, beef ribs, and salt. Simmer for 2 hours. Strain the broth into another pot, reserving the remaining ingredients to serve as a side dish or to use in other dishes.

VARIATIONS:
Fresh tortellini are traditionally cooked in this broth and served with grated Parmesan. Alternatively, small pasta shapes may be cooked and served in the same manner (children love the star shapes). If you want a thicker soup, remove the meat, and using a hand-held blender, blend the vegetables with the broth. If you prefer the soup thicker still, add an extra potato or two while cooking. Once the potatoes are soft, use a hand-held blender and blend them into the soup. The meat may be used to make Italian Potato Cakes (page 142).

Brodo di Pollo CHICKEN BROTH
Refer to the preceding Meat Broth recipe. Substitute half a chicken (2 pounds) for the beef ribs. The method is the same, as are the variations.

Brodo Vegetale VEGETABLE BROTH
Refer to the preceding Meat Broth recipe, obviously eliminating the meat. The method is the same, as are the variations.

Minestra di Verdura
VEGETABLE SOUP

6 servings – prep. 30 min. – cooking time 1 hr. (pressure cooker 20 min.)

Minestra di verdura, otherwise known as Minestrone, is an everyday favorite in Tuscany. It is satisfying on a cold winter evening, and constitutes a nourishing meal that is high in fiber. Small pasta shapes, rice, or toasted bread rounds can be added.

½ CUP EXTRA-VIRGIN OLIVE OIL
1 ONION, CHOPPED
1 CLOVE GARLIC, CHOPPED
1 STALK CELERY, CHOPPED
2 CARROTS, PEELED AND CHOPPED
2 BOILING POTATOES, PEELED AND CHOPPED
2 ZUCCHINI, CHOPPED
2 LEEKS, WASHED AND CHOPPED
½ SMALL HEAD CABBAGE, CHOPPED
1 CUBE VEGETABLE-FLAVOR STOCK
1 (8-OUNCE) CAN PLUM TOMATOES
1 (8-OUNCE) CAN CANNELLINI BEANS, DRAINED
SALT AND BLACK PEPPER

Heat the olive oil in a large lidded nonstick saucepan, and gently sauté the onion and garlic. Add all the fresh vegetables and stir well. Add enough water to cover the vegetables, the stock cube, the canned tomatoes with their juice, and the beans. Simmer, partially covered, for 1 hour, stirring occasionally. Adjust the flavor with salt and pepper, and serve.

VARIATIONS:
Add ¼ cup of pasta or rice per person, 15 minutes before the end of the cooking time.

Place a toasted slice of bread in each soup bowl, pour the steaming soup over the bread and serve.

Chicken broth may be used in place of the water and stock cube.

Minestra di Cavolfiore

CAULIFLOWER SOUP

6 servings – prep. 15 min. – cooking time 30 min. (pressure cooker 15 min.)

2 TABLESPOONS EXTRA-VIRGIN OLIVE OIL
1 ONION, CHOPPED
1 SMALL HEAD CAULIFLOWER, BROKEN INTO FLORETS
1 CUBE VEGETABLE-FLAVOR STOCK
SALT
1/2 CUP HEAVY CREAM
1/4 CUP GRATED PARMESAN CHEESE

Heat the olive oil in a large nonstick saucepan and sauté the onion until golden. Mix the cauliflower with the onion. Add the stock cube and enough water to cover the cauliflower. If you use a pressure cooker, add only 1 quart of water. Simmer gently for 30 minutes and add salt to taste. Add the cream and Parmesan. Using a hand-held blender, blend the soup.

VARIATIONS:
Chicken broth may be used in place of the stock cube and water.

You may prefer using crumbled Stilton or Gorgonzola cheese instead of the Parmesan. For extra flavor, you may also add a Parmesan rind while the soup is simmering. Remove at the end of the cooking time and discard.

Minestra di Porri e Patate
LEEK AND POTATO SOUP

6 servings – prep. 15 min. – cooking time 1 hr. (pressure cooker 15 min.)

---

2 TABLESPOONS EXTRA-VIRGIN OLIVE OIL
5 SMALL LEEKS, WASHED AND CHOPPED
6 BOILING POTATOES, PEELED AND DICED
1 CUBE VEGETABLE-FLAVOR STOCK
SALT
GORGONZOLA OR STILTON CHEESE

Heat the olive oil in a large nonstick saucepan, and gently sauté the leeks. Add the potatoes, the stock cube and enough water to cover the ingredients. Simmer for about 40 minutes or until the potatoes are soft. Using a hand-held blender, blend three-quarters of the soup, leaving the remaining quarter to add texture. Add salt to taste and serve with cheese crumbled in the soup.

VARIATION:
For added flavor, add a Parmesan rind to the pot while the soup is simmering. Remove at the end of the cooking time and discard.

Minestra di Funghi
MUSHROOM SOUP

6 servings – prep. 20 min. – cooking time 30 min. (pressure cooker 15 min.)

2 TABLESPOONS EXTRA-VIRGIN OLIVE OIL
1 ONION, CHOPPED
2 CLOVES GARLIC, CHOPPED
1 POUND FRESH PORCINI MUSHROOMS, FINELY DICED
1 POUND BUTTON MUSHROOMS, FINELY DICED
1 TABLESPOON CHOPPED FRESH PARSLEY
1 CUBE VEGETABLE-FLAVOR STOCK
1 CUP HEAVY CREAM
SALT AND BLACK PEPPER
CROUTONS AND GRATED PARMESAN CHEESE, FOR GARNISH

Heat the olive oil in a large nonstick saucepan and sauté the onion and garlic. Add the mushrooms and parsley, enough water to cover the ingredients, and the stock cube. Allow the soup to simmer for 30 minutes. Using a hand-held blender, blend the soup until smooth (leave rough if desired). Add the cream, and salt and pepper to taste. Stir well. Serve with a sprinkling of croutons and grated Parmesan.

VARIATIONS:
Chicken broth may be substituted for the water and stock cube.

If you prefer a thicker soup, at the end of the cooking time add ½ cup of water mixed with 1 tablespoon of flour. Gradually stir into the soup and bring to a boil, stirring continuously.

For extra flavor, add a Parmesan rind while the soup is simmering. Remove and discard at the end of the cooking time.

Zuppa di Cipolle
ONION SOUP

6 servings – preparation 20 min. – cooking time 30 min.

3 TABLESPOONS EXTRA-VIRGIN OLIVE OIL
1½ POUNDS WHITE ONIONS, THINLY SLICED
2 TABLESPOONS FLOUR
6 CUPS HOT WATER
1 CUBE VEGETABLE-FLAVOR STOCK
SALT AND BLACK PEPPER
6 SLICES BREAD
BUTTER
PARMESAN CHEESE, GRATED

Heat the olive oil in a large nonstick saucepan and gently sauté the onions. When the onions are translucent, add the flour, and stir in the hot water and stock cube. Add salt and pepper to taste. Simmer, uncovered, for 30 minutes. Toast the slices of bread, butter them, and cut into cubes. Serve the soup sprinkled with the Parmesan and bread cubes.

VARIATION:
Vegetable broth is our favorite substitute for the water and stock cube.

Minestra di Farro/Orzo

SPELT OR BARLEY SOUP

6 servings – preparation 20 min. – cooking time 70 min.

This soup is rich and heavenly, ideal in the winter and guaranteed to warm up anyone who dines at your table. In Tuscany, farro (spelt) was once considered a poor man's grain. Tuscans used this grain for soups in the winter and salads in the summer. Luckily, this tradition carries on today. Spelt gives soup a wonderful flavor and a unique robust texture, and in salad it is a creative change from rice or pasta (not to mention the health benefits of eating whole grain). If spelt is not available in your area, barley is a perfect substitute. This soup takes time to prepare, and it is excellent for freezing, therefore we suggest making a double batch.

---

2 TABLESPOONS EXTRA-VIRGIN OLIVE OIL, PLUS ADDITIONAL
   FOR DRIZZLING
1 ONION, FINELY SLICED
1 LARGE CARROT, PEELED AND CHOPPED
2 PLUM TOMATOES, CHOPPED
1 LARGE STALK CELERY, CHOPPED
1 TABLESPOON CHOPPED FRESH PARSLEY
$1\frac{1}{4}$ CUPS UNCOOKED SPELT OR PEARL BARLEY
1 (14-OUNCE) CAN CANNELLINI BEANS, DRAINED
8 CUPS HOT WATER
1 CUBE VEGETABLE-FLAVOR STOCK
SALT

Heat the olive oil in a large nonstick lidded saucepan and sauté the onion until translucent. Add all the other chopped vegetables and the parsley. Stir well. Add the spelt, beans, hot water, and stock cube. Stir well and add salt to taste. Simmer, partially covered, for at least an hour, stirring occasionally. The soup is ready when the spelt is soft and has absorbed enough water to have a thick consistency. Serve with a drizzle of extra-virgin olive oil.

TIP:
The cooking time can be reduced to 40 minutes by using a pressure cooker.

Minestra di Pomodoro con Riso

TOMATO AND RICE SOUP

6 servings – preparation 15 min. – cooking time 1 hr.

---

2 TABLESPOONS EXTRA-VIRGIN OLIVE OIL, PLUS EXTRA FOR
  DRIZZLING
1 ONION, FINELY CHOPPED
2 CLOVES GARLIC, FINELY CHOPPED
2 (14-OUNCE) CANS PLUM TOMATOES, CHOPPED
1 CUBE VEGETABLE-FLAVOR STOCK
2 TEASPOONS DRIED OREGANO
$1/4$ CUP CHOPPED FRESH BASIL
$1\frac{1}{4}$ CUPS UNCOOKED RICE
SALT
PARMESAN CHEESE, GRATED

Heat the olive oil in a large nonstick saucepan, and gently sauté the
onion and garlic. Add the tomatoes with their juice. Add the stock cube
and 4 cups of water. Bring to a boil. Stir in the oregano and basil. Add
the rice and simmer until tender, stirring occasionally. Add salt to taste.
Sprinkle liberally with grated Parmesan, drizzle on a small amount of
extra-virgin olive oil, and serve.

VARIATION:
Vegetable broth may be used in place of the stock cube and water.

Insalata di Tonno e Fagioli

TUNA AND BEAN SALAD

4 servings – preparation 10 min.

---

2 (8-OUNCE) CANS CANNELLINI BEANS, DRAINED AND RINSED,
  OR 1½ CUPS DRIED
3 PLUM TOMATOES, CUT INTO LARGE CHUNKS
1 SMALL ONION, FINELY CHOPPED
4 LEAVES FRESH BASIL, FINELY CHOPPED
1 (14-OUNCE) CAN TUNA, PACKED IN OLIVE OIL, DRAINED
1 TEASPOON DRIED OREGANO
SALT AND BLACK PEPPER
½ CUP OLIVE OIL

If you use dried beans, soak them overnight. The beans must be well rinsed and then cooked in a pressure cooker for 30 minutes. Otherwise, drain and rinse the canned beans before using. In a large mixing bowl, combine the beans, tomatoes, onion, basil and tuna. Add a sprinkling of oregano, and salt and pepper to taste. Add the olive oil and mix well. Place in a large salad bowl and serve.

VARIATION:
Chickpeas or lentils are suitable substitutes for the cannellini beans.

Insalata Mista

MIXED SALAD

6 servings – preparation 15 min.

There are many ways to prepare a mixed green salad. This is a simple Tuscan classic, but feel free to be creative. We enjoy using many different kinds of vegetables like bean sprouts, red, green, or yellow bell peppers, broccoli, cauliflower, fennel, spinach, and mixed greens. Fruit and nuts are also suitable alternatives: try combining chopped oranges and toasted pine nuts, or chopped grapes and walnuts with mixed greens. Another appetizing variation is a mixture of arugula, cherry tomatoes, and shavings of Parmesan cheese.

---

1 SMALL HEAD GREEN LEAF LETTUCE, CHOPPED
1 SMALL HEAD RED LETTUCE, CHOPPED
½ CUCUMBER, CUT INTO LARGE CHUNKS
3 PLUM TOMATOES, CUT INTO LARGE CHUNKS
4 GREEN ONIONS, WHOLE
10 RADISHES, WHOLE
2 CARROTS, PEELED AND GRATED
½ CUP OLIVE OIL
A DASH OF RED WINE VINEGAR
SALT

Place the lettuces, cucumber, and tomato in a large salad bowl. Add the green onions, radishes, and grated carrots. Dress with the oil, vinegar, and salt to taste.

Spiedini di Mozzarella e Pomodori
MOZZARELLA AND TOMATO KEBABS

4 servings – preparation 10 min.

These kebabs are an original and very eye-catching idea for a summer picnic or dinner party.

---

1 POUND CHERRY TOMATOES
1 (9-OUNCE) PACKAGE MINI MOZZARELLA BALLS (BOCCONCINI)
BLACK AND GREEN OLIVES, PITTED
3 TABLESPOONS OLIVE OIL
⅓ CUP CHOPPED FRESH BASIL
SALT AND BLACK PEPPER

Make the kebabs by skewering the tomatoes, mini mozzarella balls, and olives onto long wooden cocktail sticks. In a large shallow serving dish, mix the olive oil, basil, and salt and pepper to taste. Roll the kebabs in the dressing, lay on a platter, and serve.

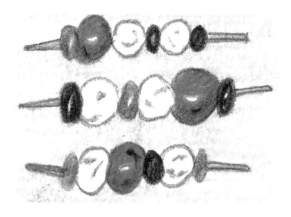

Insalata Caprese

MOZZARELLA AND TOMATO SALAD

4 servings – preparation 10 min.

The simple flavors of this salad make it an Italian classic.

---

2 (8-OUNCE) PACKAGES MOZZARELLA CHEESE, CUT INTO LARGE
    CHUNKS (SEE TIP)
8 PLUM TOMATOES, CUT INTO LARGE CHUNKS
12 LEAVES FRESH BASIL, CHOPPED
2 TEASPOONS DRIED OREGANO
SALT AND BLACK PEPPER
½ CUP OLIVE OIL

In a large mixing bowl, combine the mozzarella and tomato pieces with the basil. Add a sprinkling of oregano, and salt and pepper to taste. Add the olive oil and mix well. Transfer to a large salad bowl. Serve with a fresh crusty loaf of bread.

TIP:
We recommend using the balls of fresh mozzarella that are sold in small packages filled with water. These can be bought in delicatessans or Italian speciality shops. Otherwise, vacuum-packed pizza mozzarella can be used.

Insalata di Patate
POTATO SALAD

6 servings – preparation 20 min.

This recipe is one of our favorite mixtures. It is an extremely versatile salad and you can more or less add whatever you like.

---

6 NEW POTATOES, SCRUBBED
½ POUND GREEN BEANS
3 PLUM TOMATOES, CUT INTO CHUNKS
3 EGGS, HARD-BOILED AND CUT INTO CHUNKS
1 TABLESPOON CAPERS
1 TABLESPOON CHOPPED, PITTED OLIVES
SALT AND BLACK PEPPER TO TASTE
½ CUP OLIVE OIL
1 TABLESPOON CHOPPED FRESH PARSLEY

Cook the potatoes in boiling water. When they are soft, drain, cool, and cut them into cubes. Cook the beans in boiling water until tender. Drain, cool, and chop. (If you use a jarred variety, make sure that they are in olive oil and not vinegar, as the latter would spoil the overall flavor of the finished salad.) Combine all the ingredients in a mixing bowl, transfer to a large salad bowl, and serve.

VARIATION:
Peas or zucchini are wonderful substitutes for the beans. You may also use diced cooked ham and chopped green onion instead of capers and olives.

Insalata di Riso

COLD RICE SALAD

8 servings – preparation 30 min.

This is a great summer supper and is ideal for picnics.

1¾ CUPS PARBOILED RICE
4 HARD-BOILED EGGS, CHOPPED
⅓ CUP GRATED PECORINO OR CHEDDAR CHEESE
3 PLUM TOMATOES, CHOPPED
½ CUCUMBER, CHOPPED
1 (4-OUNCE) CAN CORN, DRAINED
1½ CUPS CHOPPED COOKED HAM
1 (8-OUNCE) CAN TUNA, PACKED IN OLIVE OIL
2 TABLESPOONS CAPERS
3 TABLESPOONS PITTED OLIVES, CHOPPED
SALT AND BLACK PEPPER
DRIED OREGANO
½ CUP OLIVE OIL

Cook the rice in salted boiling water until tender. Drain and cool. In a large salad bowl, mix the eggs, cheese, vegetables, ham, undrained tuna, capers, and olives with the rice. Add salt and pepper to taste and a sprinkling of oregano. Add the olive oil and mix well.

Pasta e Riso
PASTA AND RICE

In Italy pasta is the staple food of the Italian diet. This came about mainly due to necessity. As pre-WWII Italy was an agricultural nation, pasta was indispensable for two reasons. First, pasta is an economical way of feeding a large family. Second, it provides a quick hot meal, and the variations of savory sauces that can accompany it are endless.

In Italy, pasta is always cooked al dente, which literally means "to the tooth." In other words, it should be drained as soon as the specified cooking time is complete. As a rule, Northern Europeans and Americans tend to overcook pasta. This is generally due to the type of pasta that is available to them. In Italy, only the durum wheat variety is made. Even if this is overcooked, it doesn't become gummy. In Northern Europe and America, one usually finds the common wheat variety. This is unfortunate, for as soon as it is overcooked, it turns into a gluey mess. We strongly advise checking the packages to see which sort of wheat has been used. If possible, buy the durum wheat variety. It may cost a little more but it is well worth it.

The amount of pasta you use in cooking obviously depends on the appetites of the people you are serving. As a loose guideline, we suggest the following: If you are serving a three-course meal, two ounces per person should suffice; if you are serving a two-course meal, three ounces per person will do; if you are serving a filling plate of pasta as a meal, four ounces per person should be enough.

Italians do not add oil to the boiling water when cooking their pasta. They add salt to taste (enough that the pasta absorbs some of the flavor) and stir the pasta two or three times during the cooking time, so that it doesn't stick together or to the pot.

Pasta e Fagioli

PASTA AND BEANS

6 servings – preparation 10 min. – cooking time 40 min.

In Italy, pasta and beans is a dish known as **Lampi e Tuoni,** *meaning "thunder and lightning" (for obvious reasons). Nevertheless, this dish is so full-flavored, one is willing to take the risk.*

---

3 CUPS DRIED CANNELLINI BEANS, OR 2 (14-OUNCE) CANS
3 TABLESPOONS OLIVE OIL
3 CLOVES GARLIC, CHOPPED
1 SPRIG FRESH ROSEMARY
1 SPRIG FRESH SAGE
4 FRESH OR CANNED PLUM TOMATOES, CHOPPED
1 CUBE VEGETABLE-FLAVOR STOCK
SALT AND BLACK PEPPER
1 POUND PENNE PASTA

If you use the dried beans, soak them overnight, and cook them in a pressure cooker for 20 minutes. For those without a pressure cooker, cook the beans over medium heat for 1 hour and 15 minutes. Always use fresh water to cook them in, and discard the water that they were soaked in. If you use canned beans, rinse the beans in a colander.

Heat the oil in a large nonstick saucepan, and sauté the garlic, rosemary, and sage, until the garlic is golden. Add the chopped tomatoes and cook for 5 minutes. Remove and discard the rosemary, otherwise all the needles will come off the sprig. Add the beans, 1½ cups of water, and the stock cube. Simmer for 10 minutes, and add salt and pepper to taste.

Bring a large saucepan of salted water to a boil, and cook the pasta for the specified time on the package, drain and mix with the bean mixture.

VARIATIONS:
The pasta can also be cooked with the beans, with more water added. This means however that it needs to be stirred continuously, as it is liable to stick. We personally prefer this method, as the pasta absorbs more flavor. Chickpeas can be substituted for the beans. If you enjoy Red Hot Chile Oil (page 7), put a few drops on this dish.

Pasta con Broccoli

BROCCOLI PASTA

6 servings – preparation 10 min. – cooking time 40 min.

---

2 TABLESPOONS SALT (OR TO TASTE), FOR PASTA COOKING WATER
1 HEAD BROCCOLI, CUT INTO FLORETS
1½ POUNDS PENNE OR RIGATONI
⅓ CUP OLIVE OIL
3 CLOVES GARLIC, CHOPPED
3 HOT CHILES (OPTIONAL)

In a large nonstick saucepan of salted boiling water, cook the broccoli for 10 minutes. Add the pasta to the broccoli and cook as specified on the pasta package. (Don't worry if the broccoli is slightly overcooked, as it will coat the pasta better.)

In the meantime, heat the olive oil in a small nonstick skillet and gently sauté the chopped garlic and chiles. Be careful not to burn the garlic.

Drain the pasta and broccoli and pour the oil mixture over it. Mix and serve immediately.

Ravioli con Burro e Salvia

BUTTER AND SAGE RAVIOLI

4 servings – preparation 5 min. – cooking time 5 min.

2/3 CUP BUTTER
10 LEAVES FRESH SAGE, FINELY CHOPPED
SALT
1 POUND FRESH SPINACH AND RICOTTA RAVIOLI
PARMESAN CHEESE, GRATED

In a large nonstick saucepan, melt the butter and gently sauté the sage. Bring a large nonstick saucepan of water to a boil, and add 1 tablespoon of salt. Cook the ravioli as directed on the package, then drain and toss gently in the saucepan with the butter and sage. Serve with grated Parmesan.

Pasta con Cavolfiore

CAULIFLOWER PASTA

6 servings – preparation 10 min. – cooking time 40 min.

1 SMALL HEAD CAULIFLOWER, CUT INTO FLORETS
2 TABLESPOONS SALT (OR TO TASTE), FOR PASTA COOKING WATER
1½ POUNDS PENNE OR RIGATONI
¼ CUP OLIVE OIL
3 CLOVES GARLIC, FINELY CHOPPED
PARMESAN CHEESE, GRATED (OPTIONAL)

Bring a large saucepan of salted water to a boil, and cook the cauliflower for 10 minutes. Add the pasta to the saucepan. Cook the pasta for the specified time on the package. The flavor of the cauliflower in the water will cook into the pasta. Heat the olive oil in a large nonstick saucepan, and gently sauté the garlic. Drain the pasta and the cauliflower, and mix with the oil and garlic. Serve with grated Parmesan if desired.

Spaghetti con Aglio, Olio, e Peperoncino

GARLIC, OLIVE OIL AND HOT CHILES SPAGHETTI

4 servings – preparation 5 min. – cooking time 10 min.

This is a really quick recipe that is suitable for those who like hot, spicy flavors. You may alter the amount of garlic cloves and/or chiles to suit your tastebuds.

⅓ CUP OLIVE OIL
3 CLOVES GARLIC, CHOPPED
1 TEASPOON GROUND RED HOT CHILES
1 POUND SPAGHETTI
1 TABLESPOON SALT (OR TO TASTE), FOR PASTA COOKING WATER

Heat the olive oil in a small nonstick skillet, and gently sauté the garlic with the chiles. Be careful not to burn the garlic, as the flavor becomes bitter when this happens. When the garlic is golden, turn off the heat. Bring a large saucepan of salted water to a boil, and cook the spaghetti for the specified time on the package. Drain the pasta and toss in the saucepan with the garlic mixture. Serve immediately.

Lasagne con Ragù

MEAT LASAGNE

8 servings – preparation 30 min. – cooking time 40 min.

To make classic Italian lasagne, we suggest buying 2 pounds of fresh lasagne pasta that can be layered and baked right out of the package. It is much easier than using the dry variety that you have to boil first. We recommend making both the meat and béchamel sauce the day before you plan on preparing your lasagne, saving you valuable time in the kitchen.

DOUBLE RECIPE MEAT SAUCE (PAGE 56)
DOUBLE RECIPE BÉCHAMEL SAUCE (PAGE 54)
2 POUNDS FRESH LASAGNE PASTA
2 CUPS GRATED PARMESAN CHEESE

Preheat the oven to 350°F. In a large (14 x 10-inch) lasagne pan, start with a thin layer of meat sauce and then a thin layer of béchamel. Sprinkle with Parmesan and add a layer of pasta. Continue layering until the pan is almost full. Finish with a layer of meat sauce and grated Parmesan on top. Bake for 40 minutes, or until the top is golden. Remove from the oven and let stand for 15 minutes. Slice and serve.

Lasagne con Spinaci e Funghi
VEGETARIAN LASAGNE

8 servings – preparation 30 min. – cooking time 40 min.

We recommend making both the tomato and béchamel sauce the day before you plan on preparing your lasagne, saving you valuable time in the kitchen.

---

3 TABLESPOONS OLIVE OIL
4 CLOVES GARLIC, CHOPPED
2 CUPS BUTTON MUSHROOMS, CHOPPED
4 CUPS COOKED SPINACH, CHOPPED
DOUBLE RECIPE TOMATO SAUCE (PAGE 58)
DOUBLE RECIPE BÉCHAMEL SAUCE (PAGE 54)
2 POUNDS FRESH LASAGNE PASTA
2 CUPS GRATED PARMESAN CHEESE

Preheat the oven to 350°F. Heat the olive oil in a large nonstick skillet and sauté the garlic and mushrooms, until soft. Add the spinach and stir well. In a large (14 x 10-inch) lasagne pan, start with a thin layer of tomato sauce, then a thin layer of béchamel, and add a layer of lasagne strips. After the first layer, continue layering with the tomato sauce, béchamel, spinach and mushroom mixture, Parmesan, and lasagne strips, until the pan is almost full. Finish with a layer of the tomato sauce and grated Parmesan on top. Bake for 40 minutes, or until the top is golden. Remove from the oven and let stand for 15 minutes. Slice and serve.

Pasta e Lenticchie
PASTA AND LENTILS

6 servings – prep. 20 min. – cooking time 1 hr. (pressure cooker 30 min.)

We recommend the miniature lentils (also known as French lentils) which are the smallest and tastiest. This is a simple and extremely nutritious meal. Beans, chickpeas, and lentils are eaten regularly in Italy. They are high in fiber and iron, low in cholesterol, and an important part of a healthy, balanced Mediterranean diet.

1½ CUPS DRIED MINIATURE LENTILS, OR 2 (8-OUNCE) CANS
3 TABLESPOONS OLIVE OIL
½ SMALL ONION, CHOPPED
1 CLOVE GARLIC, CHOPPED
1 SMALL CARROT, PEELED AND FINELY CHOPPED
1 STALK CELERY, FINELY CHOPPED
2 SMALL PLUM TOMATOES, CHOPPED
½ CUBE VEGETABLE-FLAVOR STOCK
SALT AND BLACK PEPPER
1 POUND PENNE

If you use dried lentils, soak them for 8 hours, then rinse and drain. Bring a large lidded saucepan of salted water to a boil and add the (dry variety) drained lentils, cover and cook for 1 hour. If you are using a pressure cooker, cook for 15 minutes from when it starts whistling. At the end of the cooking time drain the lentils. If you use the canned variety, they are already cooked, so just rinse and drain. Heat the olive oil in a large nonstick saucepan, and sauté the onion and garlic for 3 minutes. Add the lentils, carrot, celery, tomatoes, half stock cube, and 2 cups of water. Cook uncovered over medium heat for 15 minutes. Add salt and pepper to taste.

Bring a large saucepan of salted water to a boil and cook the pasta for the specified time on the package. Drain and stir into the lentil mixture. Serve with freshly ground black pepper or a few drops of Hot Chile Oil (page 7).

Tagliatelle con Funghi e Panna
MUSHROOMS AND CREAM TAGLIATELLE

6 servings – preparation 30 min. – cooking time 15 min.

2 TABLESPOONS OLIVE OIL
2 CLOVES GARLIC, CHOPPED
1 POUND FRESH PORCINI MUSHROOMS, CHOPPED
1 POUND BUTTON MUSHROOMS, CHOPPED
1¾ CUPS HEAVY CREAM
SALT
1½ POUNDS (24 OUNCES) TAGLIATELLE

Heat the olive oil in a nonstick skillet, and sauté the garlic and the mushrooms. Cook for 15 minutes, until the mushrooms are soft. Mix in the cream and add salt to taste, stir well, and then turn off the heat. Bring a large saucepan of salted water to a boil, and cook the pasta for the specified cooking time on the package. Drain the pasta and mix with the mushroom mixture. Sprinkle with freshly grated Parmesan and serve.

VARIATIONS:
Try adding diced cooked ham or crumbled bacon to the original recipe, with a small amount of tomato sauce. Or try using ham and peas instead of mushrooms. Equally delicious and colorful.

Fusilli con Salsiccia e Verdure
ITALIAN SAUSAGE AND VEGETABLES WITH FUSILLI

6 servings – preparation 20 min. – cooking time 1 hr.

3 ITALIAN GARLIC SAUSAGES
2 TABLESPOONS OLIVE OIL
½ ONION, FINELY CHOPPED
1 CLOVE GARLIC, FINELY CHOPPED
1 CARROT, PEELED AND GRATED
1 STALK CELERY, FINELY CHOPPED
¾ CUP RED OR DRY WHITE WINE
1 (14-OUNCE) CAN PLUM TOMATOES, CHOPPED (RESERVING JUICE)
1 TABLESPOON DRIED OREGANO
2 TABLESPOONS CHOPPED FRESH BASIL
SALT AND BLACK PEPPER
1½ POUNDS (24 OUNCES) FUSILLI PASTA
½ CUP GRATED PARMESAN CHEESE

Remove the casings from the sausages and crumble them into a small nonstick skillet. Brown well, drain off any excess fat, and set aside. Heat the olive oil in a large lidded nonstick saucepan, and sauté the onion, garlic, carrot and celery, over medium heat for 5 minutes. Stir the sausages into the mixture, and add the wine. Turn the heat up and stir occasionally for 10 minutes, or until the wine has evaporated. Stir in the tomatoes and their juice. Add the oregano, basil, and salt and pepper to taste. Cover the saucepan and simmer over low heat for 1 hour, stirring occasionally. If the sauce becomes too thick during the cooking time, add a little water. At the end of the cooking time, remove the lid, and reduce the sauce to desired consistency.

Bring a large saucepan of salted water to a boil and cook the pasta for the specified time on the package. Drain and toss with the sauce. Serve with a dish of Parmesan on the side.

VARIATION:
You may also add 1 cup of chopped button mushrooms to this sauce. Put them in when sautéing the vegetables.

Pasta con Salsiccia e Peperoni
ITALIAN SAUSAGE AND PEPPERS WITH PENNE

6 servings – preparation 15 min. – cooking time 30 min.

4 TABLESPOONS OLIVE OIL
2 CLOVES GARLIC, CHOPPED
4 BELL PEPPERS, DICED
1 ONION, PEELED AND DICED
4 ITALIAN GARLIC SAUSAGES
1 (8-OUNCE) CAN PLUM TOMATOES, DRAINED AND CHOPPED
SALT AND BLACK PEPPER
1½ POUNDS (24 OUNCES) PENNE
¼ CUP GRATED PARMESAN CHEESE (OPTIONAL)

Heat the olive oil in a large nonstick saucepan, and gently sauté the garlic, peppers and onions for 5 minutes. Discard the sausage casings and crumble the sausage meat in with the vegetables. Brown and then drain off any excess fat. Add the tomatoes to the pan, and simmer gently for 30 minutes. Adjust the flavor with salt and pepper. Bring a large saucepan of salted water to a boil and cook the pasta for the specified time on the package. Drain and toss with the sausage sauce. Serve with Parmesan if desired.

Farfalle con Salmone Affumicato e Panna

SMOKED SALMON AND CREAM WITH BUTTERFLY PASTA

4 servings – preparation 10 min. – cooking time 10 min.

This is a wonderfully simple recipe and a sure winner for any dinner party. Try serving a shrimp cocktail as an appetizer, followed by this pasta, and then your favorite fish dish. We usually serve grilled fish with lemon and rosemary, salad, and a fresh crusty loaf of bread. Lemon sorbet is the perfect ending to this fabulous meal.

$\frac{2}{3}$ CUP BUTTER
$\frac{2}{3}$ CUP SMOKED SALMON, CUT INTO SMALL PIECES
1 TABLESPOON WHISKEY
$\frac{3}{4}$ CUP HEAVY CREAM
SALT
1 POUND BUTTERFLY (BOWTIE) PASTA

Melt the butter in a nonstick saucepan over medium heat, and mix in the salmon. Add the whiskey and stir, until it has evaporated. Add the cream and stir gently until heated through. Adjust the flavor with a little salt, if necessary. Bring a large saucepan of salted water to a boil and cook the pasta for the specified time on the package, and drain. Mix the pasta with the sauce, and serve immediately.

VARIATION:
Half an onion may be chopped and sautéed in the butter, prior to adding the salmon.

Penne con Zucchine Gratinate

PENNE WITH ZUCCHINI GRATIN

4 servings – preparation 10 min. – cooking time 30 min.

¼ CUP OLIVE OIL
4 ZUCCHINI, THINLY SLICED
½ ONION, THINLY SLICED
SALT
1 POUND PENNE
3 EGGS, HARD-BOILED AND DICED
8 OUNCES MOZZARELLA CHEESE, DICED
⅓ CUP GRATED PARMESAN CHEESE

Preheat the oven to 350°F. Heat the olive oil in a large nonstick saucepan, and gently sauté the zucchini and onion until soft. Add salt to taste. Bring a large saucepan of salted water to a boil and cook the pasta for 7 minutes and drain. The pasta will finish cooking in the oven. Combine all of the ingredients except the Parmesan and put in a (12 x 9-inch) greased ovenproof dish. Sprinkle the grated Parmesan over the top and then bake for 15 minutes.

Risotto con Asparagi

ASPARAGUS RISOTTO

6 servings – preparation 15 min. – cooking time 50 min.

2 QUARTS VEGETABLE OR CHICKEN BROTH
¼ CUP OLIVE OIL
1 SMALL ONION, FINELY CHOPPED
10 ASPARAGUS SPEARS, CHOPPED
2⅓ CUPS ARBORIO RICE
¾ CUP WHITE WINE
SALT AND BLACK PEPPER
1 TABLESPOON BUTTER
½ CUP GRATED PARMESAN CHEESE

In a saucepan, bring the broth to a boil. Meanwhile heat the olive oil in another large nonstick saucepan and sauté the onion until it is transparent. Add the chopped asparagus to the onion and continue to sauté for 3 minutes. Add the rice to the asparagus and onion, and mix well to coat the rice. Add the white wine. Let the wine reduce and then gradually start adding ladlefuls of hot broth, cooking after each addition until the liquid is reduced, stirring continuously. After 20 minutes the rice will be cooked. The risotto is ready when the rice has absorbed the broth and is plump and tender. Add salt and pepper to taste, and stir in the butter. Sprinkle liberally with Parmesan and serve.

VARIATION:
Instead of the broth, you can also use 2 quarts of water heated with the correct quantity of stock cubes for that measurement of liquid.

Risotto ai Funghi
MUSHROOM RISOTTO

6 servings – preparation 15 min. – cooking time 40 min.

2 TABLESPOONS OLIVE OIL
1 ONION, FINELY CHOPPED
1 CLOVE GARLIC, LEFT WHOLE
2 QUARTS VEGETABLE OR CHICKEN BROTH
1 POUND FRESH PORCINI OR BUTTON MUSHROOMS, FINELY
    CHOPPED
1½ TABLESPOONS CHOPPED FRESH PARSLEY
SALT AND BLACK PEPPER
2 QUARTS VEGETABLE OR CHICKEN BROTH
2⅓ CUPS ARBORIO RICE
½ CUP GRATED PARMESAN CHEESE
1 TABLESPOON BUTTER

Heat the olive oil in a large nonstick saucepan, and sauté the onion and whole garlic clove until the onion is soft and the garlic clove is golden. In a separate saucepan, bring the broth to a boil. Remove and discard the garlic clove and stir in the mushrooms and 1 tablespoon of parsley. Sauté for 5 minutes, and add salt and pepper to taste. Add the rice to the mushroom mixture, and stir well to coat the rice. Gradually start adding ladlefuls of hot broth, cooking after each addition until the liquid is reduced, stirring continuously. After 20 minutes the rice will be cooked. The broth at this point will have absorbed into the rice, leaving a rich sauce. Stir in the butter and Parmesan. Serve with a sprinkling of finely chopped parsley.

VARIATION:
Instead of the broth, you can also use 2 quarts of water heated with the correct quantity of stock cubes for that measurement of liquid.

Risotto con la Zucca

PUMPKIN RISOTTO

6 servings – preparation 10 min. – cooking time 40 min.

¼ CUP OLIVE OIL
1 ONION, FINELY CHOPPED
3 LEAVES FRESH SAGE, CHOPPED
1 CLOVE GARLIC, LEFT WHOLE
1 POUND FRESH PUMPKIN OR WINTER SQUASH, CUBED
2 QUARTS VEGETABLE BROTH
2⅓ CUPS ARBORIO RICE
SALT
⅓ CUP BUTTER
½ CUP GRATED PARMESAN CHEESE
BLACK PEPPER

Heat the olive oil in a large nonstick saucepan, and sauté the onion, sage, and garlic for 5 minutes, or until the onion is transparent. Add the pumpkin and mix well. In a separate saucepan, bring the broth to a boil. Cover the pan that contains the pumpkin mixture and cook for 10 minutes over medium heat. Uncover, remove and discard the clove of garlic, and gently mash the soft pumpkin into a purée. Add the rice and salt to taste, then gradually start adding ladlefuls of hot broth, cooking after each addition until the liquid is reduced, stirring continuously. After 20 minutes, the rice will be cooked. The broth at this point will have absorbed into the rice, leaving a rich sauce. Stir in the butter, and serve with a generous sprinkling of Parmesan and black pepper.

VARIATION:
Instead of the broth, you can also use 2 quarts of water heated with the correct quantity of stock cubes for that measurement of liquid.

Risotto agli Zucchini
ZUCCHINI RISOTTO

6 servings – preparation 15 min. – cooking time 20 min.

2 TABLESPOONS OLIVE OIL
1 ONION, FINELY CHOPPED
4 MEDIUM ZUCCHINI, FINELY GRATED
¾ CUP DRY WHITE WINE
2⅓ CUPS ARBORIO RICE
2 QUARTS VEGETABLE OR CHICKEN BROTH
SALT AND BLACK PEPPER
1 TABLESPOON BUTTER
½ CUP GRATED PARMESAN CHEESE

Heat the olive oil in a large nonstick saucepan, and sauté the onion until soft. Add the zucchini. Cook for 10 minutes over medium heat, and then add the wine. Cook until the wine has evaporated. Stir in the rice. In a separate saucepan, bring the broth to a boil. Gradually start adding ladlefuls of hot broth to the rice, cooking after each addition until the liquid is reduced, stirring continuously. Add salt and pepper to taste. After 20 minutes the rice will be cooked. The broth will have been absorbed, creating a scrumptious sauce. Add the butter and freshly grated Parmesan, and mix well.

VARIATION:
Instead of the broth, you can also use 2 quarts of water heated with the correct quantity of stock cubes for that measurement of liquid.

Salse

SAUCES

In this chapter we are pleased to include a delightful variety of savory sauces. The principle of Italian cuisine, simple yet expertly combined ingredients, culminates in the way Italians create richly flavored sauces. They cook with an inborn instinct, and this irresistible selection is yet another example of their ingenuity in the kitchen.

Besciamella
BÉCHAMEL SAUCE

2 ³/₄ cups – preparation 5 min. – cooking time 10 min.

---

¹/₃ CUP BUTTER
¹/₃ CUP ALL-PURPOSE FLOUR
2 CUPS WHOLE MILK
SALT AND BLACK PEPPER
1 TEASPOON GROUND NUTMEG

In a medium-size nonstick saucepan, melt the butter over low heat. Turn off the heat. Gradually add the flour, stirring continuously, and once blended, gradually whisk in the milk until smooth. Over medium heat bring to a boil, stirring continuously. Once the sauce is boiling, continue stirring for 2 minutes. Add salt, pepper, and nutmeg to taste.

Salsa di Limone
LEMON SAUCE

¹/₂ cup – preparation 5 min.

Add a touch of class to your favorite fish dish. Drizzle this mouthwatering sauce over the fish, decorate with thin slices of lemon and fresh parsley, and serve. This sauce is also ideal for basting fish cooked on the barbecue.

JUICE OF 2 LEMONS, STRAINED
2 TABLESPOONS CHOPPED FRESH CHIVES
¹/₃ CUP OLIVE OIL
SALT AND BLACK PEPPER TO TASTE

Combine all the ingredients.

Prosciutto Cotto e Piselli

PEA AND HAM SAUCE

Refer to our Peas and Ham recipe (page 140): This vegetable dish also makes a wonderful pasta sauce. Prepare penne and once cooked, mix with the vegetables and serve. This dish makes 4 servings (1 pound penne).

Pesto alla Genovese

PESTO

Refer to our Pesto Crostini recipe (page 14): this classic recipe, quick and easy to prepare, creates a delicate flavor that is sure to please. We recommend serving pesto with spaghetti. Once cooked and tossed with the sauce, decorate with some whole toasted pine nuts, grated Parmesan, and a fresh basil leaf. This recipe makes enough pesto for 6 servings (1½ pounds spaghetti).

Zucchini del Basilico e Pomodoro

TOMATO AND BASIL ZUCCHINI SAUCE

Refer to our Tomato and Basil Zucchini recipe (page 149): this vegetable dish also makes a wonderful pasta sauce. Prepare penne, and once cooked, mix with the vegetables and serve. This dish makes 8 servings (2 pounds penne).

Ragù
MEAT SAUCE

5 cups – preparation 40 min. – cooking time 2 hr.

This sauce is suitable to serve with tagliatelle or other pastas. It is also excellent in lasagne or crêpes.

1½ TABLESPOONS OLIVE OIL
⅓ CUP BUTTER
2 ONIONS, CHOPPED
3 STALKS CELERY, CHOPPED
3 LARGE CARROTS, PEELED AND CHOPPED
1 POUND GROUND BEEF
1 TABLESPOON SALT
1 TABLESPOON BLACK PEPPER
1 CUP RED OR DRY WHITE WINE
1 (14-OUNCE) CAN PLUM TOMATOES, CHOPPED (RESERVING JUICE)
2 TEASPOONS GROUND NUTMEG

Heat the oil and butter in a large nonstick lidded saucepan over medium heat and sauté the vegetables for 5 minutes. Stir in the ground beef, salt, and pepper. Cook for 15 minutes, or until the beef is no longer pink. Add the wine and simmer for 10 minutes, or until it is completely evaporated, stirring occasionally. Add the tomatoes and their juice, the nutmeg, and stir well. Simmer gently for 2 hours, partially covered. Stir occasionally and add a little water during the cooking time, if the sauce becomes too thick.

TIPS:
The longer you simmer this sauce, the more full-bodied the flavor becomes. Therefore, if you have time, you may let the sauce simmer, partially covered, for 3 hours (as opposed to 2 hours). Stir occasionally, adding a little water during the cooking time, if necessary. As this sauce requires a fair amount of preparation and cooking time, we suggest making a double recipe and freezing half of it.

VARIATIONS:

The celery may be replaced with red and yellow bell peppers.

For another variation, add two Italian garlic sausages. Remove the casings and crumble the sausage meat into a skillet. Cook well and drain off the excess fat. Mix the sausages and ½ cup black olives into the sauce at the end of the cooking time.

Pomarola

TOMATO AND VEGETABLE SAUCE

5 cups – preparation 15 min. – cooking time 1 hr.

This sauce is very light, as there is no frying required. When serving, a small amount of extra-virgin olive oil can be drizzled over the pasta, giving it a unique flavor.

---

1 ONION, FINELY CHOPPED
2 CLOVES GARLIC, FINELY CHOPPED
1 CARROT, PEELED AND FINELY CHOPPED
1 STALK CELERY, FINELY CHOPPED
1 TABLESPOON CHOPPED FRESH PARSLEY
2 TABLESPOONS CHOPPED FRESH BASIL
2 (14-OUNCE) CANS PLUM TOMATOES, CHOPPED (RESERVING JUICE)
SALT

Place all the vegetables in a large saucepan with the canned tomatoes and their juice. Add 2 cups of water and salt to taste. Bring to a boil and then simmer over low heat for 1 hour.

Sugo di Pomodoro
TOMATO SAUCE

4 cups – preparation 10 min. – cooking time 40 min.

This is probably the most popular and at the same time the most basic of Italian sauces. It is easy to prepare and very versatile. When cool, it can be kept for up to five days in the fridge. It also freezes well, and therefore may be used at a later date.

---

2 TABLESPOONS OLIVE OIL
1 SMALL ONION, FINELY CHOPPED
2 CLOVES GARLIC, FINELY CHOPPED
2 (14-OUNCE) CANS PLUM TOMATOES, CHOPPED (RESERVING JUICE)
3 TABLESPOONS CHOPPED FRESH BASIL
SALT
1 TABLESPOON DRIED OREGANO (OPTIONAL)

Heat the olive oil in a large nonstick saucepan, and sauté the onion and garlic until golden. Add the tomatoes with their juice, basil, salt to taste, and oregano, if using. Add 2 cups of water and bring to a boil. Simmer over low heat for 40 minutes, stirring occasionally.

VARIATIONS:
Dice 8 ounces of mozzarella cheese. When the pasta has been mixed with the tomato sauce, stir in the mozzarella and serve at once.

Ricotta cheese (8 ounces) may also be mixed with the sauce and pasta and makes a nice change.

Fish Sauce: Create a mouthwatering fish sauce, by adding a 4-ounce can of drained tuna, 4 finely chopped anchovy fillets, 3 tablespoons of chopped capers, and 3 tablespoons of fresh chopped parsley to the sauce.

Eggplant Sauce: Again using the tomato sauce as a base, a delectable eggplant sauce can be achieved. Finely chop a small eggplant and sauté in olive oil until soft and golden. Drain off any excess oil and mix the eggplant with the tomato sauce.

By adding pitted olives or capers to the tomato sauce, another sauce is obtained. This is not only popular in Tuscany, but also in the southern region of Puglia, where everyone picks and bottles his own olives and capers.

A tomato cream sauce can also be made by adding ¾ cup of heavy cream to the tomato sauce. This is also delicious if you sauté three finely chopped cloves of garlic, prior to adding the tomato sauce and the cream to the pan.

Another variation is to sauté a finely chopped onion and ½ cup of crumbled bacon. When the onion is soft and the bacon is browned, mix with the tomato sauce.

Carne
MEAT

The creativity of Italians is truly demonstrated in their culinary ability. The way in which meat is prepared, cooked and presented is yet another fine example of this talent. Whether pot or oven roasted, they combine simple methods with the freshest of ingredients to compliment each selected cut of meat, bringing out the most of the flavor, aroma and succulent tenderness.

Lesso Rifatto
BEEF AND ONIONS

6 servings – preparation 10 min. – cooking time 20 min.

This is a traditional Tuscan dish that was developed as a way of tenderizing and enjoying a cheaper cut of meat. First, meat is used to make a broth for soup, then this dish is served as a second course, following the soup. A quick and simple solution for any busy weekday supper.

---

2 POUNDS BOILED BEEF RIB (FROM MEAT BROTH, PAGE 20)
2 TABLESPOONS OLIVE OIL
3 LARGE ONIONS, FINELY CHOPPED
4 CANNED PLUM TOMATOES, CHOPPED
SALT AND BLACK PEPPER

Trim the meat of all fat, bones, and gristle. Cut into thin strips. Heat the olive oil in a nonstick saucepan, and sauté the onions until soft. Add the beef strips, tomatoes, and salt and pepper to taste. Cover and cook for 10 minutes, allowing all the flavors to blend. Serve with crusty bread.

Stracotto
BEEF POT ROAST

6 servings – preparation 30 min. – cooking time 1 hr. and 30 min.

2 POUNDS BEEF BRISKET, CHUCK, OR SIRLOIN
KITCHEN TWINE
5 TABLESPOONS OLIVE OIL
1 LARGE ONION, COARSELY CHOPPED
1 LARGE CARROT, PEELED AND COARSELY CHOPPED
2 STALKS CELERY, COARSELY CHOPPED
4 BAY LEAVES
¾ CUP RED WINE
SALT AND BLACK PEPPER
½ CUBE BEEF-FLAVOR STOCK

Tie up the meat with the kitchen twine, so that it will remain compact during the cooking time. In a large nonstick pan, heat the oil and brown the meat on all sides. Add the vegetables and the bay leaves, and sauté for 10 minutes. Add the red wine, and salt and pepper to taste. Cook uncovered until the wine reduces completely. Add 1½ cups of water and the stock cube half, cover partially, and simmer for 1 hour and 30 minutes. At the end of this time, the water will have evaporated and the meat will be very tender. Remove the string and carve the beef. Arrange the slices on a warm serving dish. Using a hand-held blender, blend the pan juices and vegetables to make a gravy, and pour over the beef. Serve with roasted potatoes.

Involtini di Manzo

BEEF ROLLS

6 servings – preparation 15 min. – cooking time 2 hr.

6 SMALL CARROTS, PEELED
6 THIN SLICES SIRLOIN STEAK
SALT AND BLACK PEPPER
6 SLICES MORTADELLA OR COOKED HAM
6 SLICES FONTINA CHEESE
KITCHEN TWINE
3 TABLESPOONS OLIVE OIL
2 CLOVES GARLIC, CHOPPED
1 POUND FRESH PORCINI OR BUTTON MUSHROOMS, CHOPPED

Boil the carrots for 15 minutes. Lay the steaks on a clean surface and sprinkle with salt and pepper to taste. Place a slice of mortadella on each slice. Add a cooked carrot to each, along with a slice of cheese. Roll up the slices and tie them with kitchen string. Heat the olive oil in a large nonstick lidded saucepan, gently sauté the garlic and mushrooms. Add the beef rolls, and sprinkle with salt and pepper to taste. Brown the beef rolls and then add ¾ cup of water to the pan. Cover and cook over low heat for 2 hours, stirring occasionally and adding water as needed (allow the water to reduce during the cooking time; stir and add ¾ cup of water each time it evaporates). At the end of the cooking time, uncover and allow any remaining water to reduce. At this point, the rolls will be very tender and surrounded by mushrooms delicately flavored with the meat juices.

TIP:

As with many meat recipes, the tenderness of the meat in this dish depends not only on the quality of the cut but also on the cooking time. Two hours on a slow simmer should suffice but you may cook it a little longer if you like.

VARIATION:

You may replace the beef with boneless turkey or chicken breast, in which case, the cooking time will be 1 hour.

Bistecca alla Fiorentina

FLORENTINE BEEF STEAK

2 servings – preparation 30 min. – cooking time 12 min.

This is undoubtedly the king of the Tuscan table. Florentine beef is famous worldwide for its flavor and size. The Chianina breed of cattle is native to Tuscany, and many believe that this breed produces the best meat for steaks. However, Tuscans will eat steaks that come from other breeds of European cattle if Chianina is not readily available.

This is not the kind of steak that can be cooked in a pan! It needs to be seared and grilled over red-hot embers and eaten rare. If you should use a steak that has been frozen, it must be completely thawed before putting it on the grill.

---

1 (2-POUND) T-BONE STEAK, 1½ TO 2 INCHES THICK
SALT AND BLACK PEPPER
EXTRA-VIRGIN OLIVE OIL

Prepare a charcoal or wood barbecue well in advance. When the coals or embers are red hot, place a grill over them for 10 minutes. The grill must be red hot before you put the steak on it. Place the steak on the grill and cook for 6 minutes (be careful that any fat dripping from the steak does not create a live flame that touches the meat). Turn the steak over and grill the other side for 6 minutes. The steak should only be turned once during the cooking time. Place the steak on a serving plate and season with salt, black pepper, and a drizzle of extra-virgin olive oil. Serve with sautéed potatoes and a salad.

Spezzatino

BEEF STEW

6 servings – prep. 20 min. – cooking time 2 hr. (pressure cooker 40 min.)

½ CUP FLOUR
2 POUNDS STEW BEEF, CUT INTO CHUNKS
¼ CUP OLIVE OR VEGETABLE OIL
3 ONIONS, CHOPPED
4 CARROTS, PEELED AND CHOPPED
2 STALKS CELERY, CHOPPED
6 BOILING POTATOES, PEELED AND CHOPPED
2 TEASPOONS DRIED OREGANO
2 TEASPOONS CHOPPED FRESH BASIL
2 (14-OUNCE) CANS PLUM TOMATOES
SALT AND BLACK PEPPER

Coat the beef in flour, and brown in an oiled, nonstick skillet. Transfer to a nonstick, heavy-bottomed saucepan and add the vegetables, herbs, and tomatoes with their juice. Add enough water to cover the contents in the pan. Stir well, and add salt and pepper to taste. Simmer over the lowest possible temperature for 2 hours, stirring occasionally. Allow the water to reduce during the cooking time. When the cooking time is complete, the water will have reduced to leave a thick gravy. Taste the beef. It should be very tender. If not, leave the stew to simmer an extra 30 minutes (add a little more water if required). Serve with a loaf of crusty bread.

Petto di Pollo con Cipolle

CHICKEN BREASTS WITH ONIONS

6 servings – preparation 15 min. – cooking time 40 min.

1½ POUNDS BONELESS CHICKEN BREASTS, THINLY SLICED
½ CUP FLOUR, SEASONED WITH SALT AND PEPPER
4 TABLESPOONS OLIVE OIL
5 LARGE WHITE ONIONS, THINLY SLICED
⅓ CUP WHITE WINE
1 CUBE CHICKEN-FLAVOR STOCK
SALT AND BLACK PEPPER

Dredge the chicken slices in seasoned flour. Heat the oil in a nonstick pan and gently brown the chicken. Add the onions to the pan and gently sauté for 10 minutes, until they have softened. Add the wine and simmer for 10 minutes. When the wine has almost evaporated, add ¾ cup of water and the stock cube. Stir gently until the stock cube has dissolved. Cover the pan and gently simmer for 30 minutes, turning the chicken occasionally. Add salt and pepper to taste. At the end of the cooking time, the chicken will be covered in a thick onion sauce. Serve with thick slices of crusty bread, roasted potatoes, or rice.

VARIATIONS:
A tasty option is to substitute button mushrooms for some of the onions. Use a small, thinly sliced onion and ½ pound of button mushrooms. Add the wine, and only ¼ cup of water, as the mushrooms release a lot of liquid. Proceed with the recipe as directed above.

Yet another variation is to use dry porcini mushrooms. Fill a small saucepan with water to the three-quarter mark and add 2 cups of dried mushrooms. Simmer for 30 minutes. Remove the mushrooms with a slotted spoon and chop. Spread over the browned chicken. Filter the cooking water through a strainer lined with paper towel or cheese cloth, and pour this juice over the chicken. Simmer gently, partially covered, for 1 hour. Stir occasionally and add water if your sauce starts to dry out before the required cooking time. Add ⅓ cup of heavy cream, salt to taste, and stir well.

(continued)

Another option is to cover each of the chicken breasts with a thin slice of cured ham and a thin slice of Fontina cheese. Once the cheese just before the end of the cooking time has melted, serve immediately. Use only about ⅓ cup of the water, plus the stock cube.

In the original recipe, the onions may be replaced with leeks or shallots.

A tomato-based cream sauce is not only another variation but also a classic in its own right. Gently sauté 3 cloves of garlic, pour 1½ cups of tomato sauce and ⅓ cup of heavy cream over the garlic, and stir well. Add this mixture to the pot of browned chicken and add salt to taste. Sprinkle with oregano if desired and simmer gently, covering the pan, for 30 minutes. Stir occasionally and at the end of the cooking time, uncover the pan and reduce the sauce to desired consistency.

Try adding tomato sauce and ⅓ cup of water to the browned chicken breasts. Season with oregano and a little salt. Add a few capers and olives. Simmer, uncovered, for 30 minutes. At the end of the cooking time, add a slice of mozzarella to the top of each chicken breast. Melt and serve with white rice or a crusty loaf of bread. This recipe also works well with thinly sliced boneless beef (brown well on both sides without the flour). Italians call this dish *pollo* (or *manzo*) *alla pizzaiola*.

The last and most obvious option is to replace the chicken with boneless turkey.

Pollo con i Peperoni
CHICKEN WITH BELL PEPPERS

4 servings – preparation 20 min. – cooking time 40 min.

¼ CUP OLIVE OIL
2 POUNDS SKINLESS CHICKEN PARTS (8 PIECES)
2 LARGE RED BELL PEPPERS, SEEDED AND THICKLY SLICED
2 LARGE GREEN BELL PEPPERS, SEEDED AND THICKLY SLICED
3 CLOVES GARLIC, CHOPPED
SALT AND BLACK PEPPER
10 CAPERS AND 10 OLIVES (OPTIONAL)

Heat the olive oil in a nonstick pan and gently brown the chicken. Add the peppers and garlic. Stir and add salt and pepper to taste. Move the peppers to the bottom of the pan and the chicken to the top. Cook over medium heat for about 30 minutes, stirring frequently. At the end of the cooking time, capers and olives can be added, if desired. Serve with slices of crusty bread or rice.

Pollo Arrosto con Aglio e Erbe

ROASTED CHICKEN WITH GARLIC AND HERBS

4 servings – preparation 15 min. – cooking time 1 hr. and 15 min.

---

1 (2-POUND) CHICKEN, RINSED AND PATTED DRY
6 CLOVES GARLIC, PEELED
3 SPRIGS FRESH ROSEMARY
6 FRESH SAGE LEAVES
3 TABLESPOONS OLIVE OIL
SALT AND BLACK PEPPER

Preheat the oven to 425°F. Place the herbs and cloves of garlic in the cavity of the chicken. Baste with the oil, and season well with salt and pepper. Place in the oven and baste every 15 minutes, until cooked. The chicken should be tender when pierced with a fork. Place on a serving platter and pour the pan juices over the roasted bird.

VARIATIONS:
If you prefer a crispier chicken, at the end of the cooking time turn on the broiler and brown on all sides.

Potatoes, carrots, and onions go well with this dish, and as they can be added to the roasting pan, they make for an easy meal. Mix them with a little olive oil (enough to lightly coat them), salt, sage, and rosemary, and arrange them around the chicken. Remember to turn the vegetables whenever you are basting the chicken.

Costolette d'Agnello al Pomodoro

LAMB CHOPS IN TOMATO SAUCE

6 servings – preparation 15 min. – cooking time 40 min.

6 SLICES BACON, CHOPPED
2 TABLESPOONS OLIVE OIL
6 (2 POUNDS) LAMB CHOPS
2 CLOVES GARLIC, WHOLE
1 SPRIG FRESH ROSEMARY
1 (14-OUNCE) CAN PLUM TOMATOES
SALT AND BLACK PEPPER

Cook the bacon until brown and crispy. Set aside to cool. Heat the olive oil in a saucepan, and sauté the lamb chops over high heat. When browned, drain any excess fat and lower the heat. Gently sauté the garlic cloves and rosemary, until the garlic is lightly colored. Add the tomatoes. Crumble the bacon into the pan. Add salt and pepper to taste and simmer for about 30 minutes or until the sauce has reduced by half. Remove the sprig of rosemary and place the chops on a warm serving plate. Pour the sauce over the chops and serve.

Arrosto d'Agnello con Patate
ROAST LEG OF LAMB WITH POTATOES

6 servings – preparation 20 min. – cooking time 2 hr.

¼ CUP OLIVE OIL
1 (2-POUND) LEG OF LAMB
5 LARGE ROASTING POTATOES, PEELED AND CUT INTO
   BITE-SIZE PIECES
½ POUND CHERRY TOMATOES
1 MEDIUM ONION, SLICED
1 TABLESPOON CHOPPED FRESH ROSEMARY
1 TABLESPOON CHOPPED FRESH THYME
1 TABLESPOON DRIED OREGANO
SALT AND BLACK PEPPER

Preheat the oven to 350°F. Pour the olive oil into a deep roasting pan. Place the leg of lamb in the center and surround it with the potatoes, tomatoes, and onion. Sprinkle with the herbs, and salt and pepper to taste. Cover the pan with foil and bake for 1 hour. After the hour is up, uncover, and stir the potatoes and tomatoes. Turn over the lamb and roast for another hour, uncovered, raising the temperature to 400°F for the last 20 minutes.

Polpette di Macinato

TUSCAN MEATBALLS

6 servings – preparation 15 min. – cooking time 45 min.

1 ONION, FINELY CHOPPED
1 CUP FINELY CHOPPED COOKED HAM OR MORTADELLA
1 CARROT, PEELED AND GRATED
1 POUND LEAN GROUND BEEF
$1/4$ CUP GRATED PARMESAN CHEESE
2 EGGS
$1/2$ CUP DRY BREAD CRUMBS
SALT AND BLACK PEPPER
$1/2$ CUP FLOUR
3 TABLESPOONS OLIVE OIL
2 CLOVES GARLIC, CHOPPED
2 CUPS TOMATO SAUCE (PAGE 58)

In a large mixing bowl, combine the onion, ham, carrot, beef, Parmesan, eggs, bread crumbs, and salt and pepper to taste. Mold into small balls (each the size of a golf ball) and roll them in the flour. Heat the olive oil in a large nonstick skillet over medium heat, and brown the meatballs. Add the garlic. Sauté gently for a couple of minutes. Add the tomato sauce and salt and pepper to taste, and simmer, uncovered, for 45 minutes, add a little water if the sauce reduces too quickly, and stir occasionally.

Costolette di Maiale con Salvia e Chianti

PORK CHOPS WITH SAGE AND CHIANTI

4 servings – preparation 20 min. – cooking time 1 hr.

¼ CUP OLIVE OIL
4 PORK CHOPS
2 CLOVES GARLIC, CHOPPED
1 TABLESPOON CHOPPED FRESH PARSLEY
3 TABLESPOONS CHOPPED FRESH SAGE
1 (8-OUNCE) CAN PLUM TOMATOES
¾ CUP CHIANTI WINE
SALT AND BLACK PEPPER TO TASTE

Heat the olive oil in a large nonstick skillet and brown the chops on both sides. Add the garlic, along with the parsley and sage and sauté gently. When the garlic is golden, add the tomatoes, red wine, and salt and pepper. Cover the pan and simmer for approximately 1 hour, turning the chops occasionally. If time allows, leave the pork chops to simmer even longer. Add a little water as the sauce reduces. They become very tender during the extended cooking time. At the end of the cooking time, transfer the chops to a warm serving plate and stir the remaining pan juices. Spoon over the chops and serve with rice or potatoes and your favorite vegetable.

Arista al Latte

PORK LOIN BRAISED IN MILK

6 servings – preparation 10 min. – cooking time 2 hr.

This recipe originates from Emilia-Romagna. Our friend Simona lives in this region, and she testifies that this is the easiest and most delectable way of cooking pork. We often serve this dish for dinner parties and it is always a great success.

---

1 (2-POUND) PORK LOIN
KITCHEN TWINE
¼ CUP OLIVE OIL
SALT AND BLACK PEPPER
1 QUART WHOLE MILK, PLUS MORE IF NECESSARY

Tie the pork loin with the kitchen twine. Heat the olive oil in a deep nonstick saucepan and thoroughly brown the pork. Add salt and pepper to taste and 2 cups of the milk, and simmer gently, uncovered, for 1 hour. Add small amounts of milk if necessary, to keep the pork moist. After the hour is up, add the remaining milk. Cover the pot and simmer gently for 1 more hour, turning the pork occasionally. At the end of the second hour, test the pork with a meat fork. Test every 15 minutes, until the pork is cooked. The fork should pierce the meat easily and the meat juices should run clear. When the pork is cooked, remove from the saucepan and reduce the remaining sauce, for about 10 minutes. The sauce will be a light brown gravy color and the milk will have congealed slightly. Remove from the heat, and using a hand-held blender, blend the sauce until smooth. Slice the pork and lay it on a warm serving plate. Pour the sauce over the meat and serve. This dish is tasty served with roasted potatoes and vegetables.

Salsicce e Fagioli

TUSCAN SAUSAGE AND CANNELLINI BEANS

4 servings – preparation 10 min. – cooking time 30 min.

This is a great weeknight dish that children enjoy.

$2\frac{1}{3}$ CUPS DRIED CANNELLINI BEANS, OR 2 (14-OUNCE) CANS
8 TUSCAN OR ITALIAN GARLIC SAUSAGES
3 TABLESPOONS OLIVE OIL
6 FRESH SAGE LEAVES
1 SPRIG FRESH ROSEMARY
4 CLOVES GARLIC, PEELED
1 CUP TOMATO SAUCE (PAGE 58), OR 4 FRESH PLUM TOMATOES

If you are using dried beans, soak them overnight. Then cook them in fresh water in a covered pot on the stove top, over medium heat for 1 hour or until tender, or in a pressure cooker for 25 minutes. Drain. If you are using the canned variety, drain and rinse. In a nonstick pan, brown the sausages and then drain off the excess grease. Lower the heat, add the olive oil, the herbs and whole garlic cloves and gently sauté. Remove the sprigs of rosemary and sage, and add the tomato sauce or fresh tomatoes. Add the beans, stir gently, and simmer for 15 minutes. We suggest serving with a fresh crusty loaf of bread.

TIP:
As Tuscan and Italian sausages are generally quite salty, we don't add extra salt to this dish. If you are using another variety of sausage, add salt to taste.

Tacchino Mediterraneo

MEDITERRANEAN TURKEY

6 servings – preparation 20 min. – cooking time 40 min.

½ CUP FLOUR
6 THIN SLICES (2 POUNDS) BONELESS TURKEY BREAST
¼ CUP OLIVE OIL
½ LARGE ONION, FINELY CHOPPED
1 LARGE CARROT, PEELED AND FINELY CHOPPED
2 STALKS CELERY, FINELY CHOPPED
2 SMALL ZUCCHINI, FINELY CHOPPED
3 CLOVES GARLIC, FINELY CHOPPED
¾ CUP DRY WHITE WINE
1 (8-OUNCE) CAN PLUM TOMATOES
2 TABLESPOONS CHOPPED FRESH BASIL
2 TABLESPOONS DRIED OREGANO
SALT AND BLACK PEPPER

Dredge the turkey with flour. Heat half of the olive oil in a large nonstick pan, and brown the turkey on both sides. Remove from the pan. Preheat the oven to 350°F. Add the other half of the olive oil to the pan and heat. Sauté all the vegetables until tender, for about 15 minutes. Add the white wine and simmer for 5 minutes. Add the tomatoes with their juice, and the basil and oregano. Stir well, until smooth. Adjust the flavor with salt and pepper. In a large baking dish, pour a layer of sauce on the bottom, lay the turkey over the top, and cover with the remaining sauce. Cover and bake for 40 minutes.

Tacchino Arrotolato

TURKEY ROLL

8 servings – preparation 30 min. – cooking time 2 hr.

This dish is a little on the long side to prepare, but we think it is well worth the effort. It is very attractive and thus good for serving at dinner parties. We have also found it successful with children who are difficult eaters. Turkey often dries out while cooking, especially if it has been roasted, but in this case, we guarantee the most tender and moist turkey you will ever sink your teeth into!

---

1 (2-POUND) TURKEY BREAST
SALT AND BLACK PEPPER
3 THIN SLICES COOKED HAM
3 THIN SLICES FONTINA CHEESE
2 CANNED ARTICHOKE HEARTS, DRAINED
1 ITALIAN GARLIC SAUSAGE
½ CUP FLOUR, SEASONED WITH SALT AND PEPPER
¼ CUP OLIVE OIL
1 SPRIG OF FRESH ROSEMARY
6 FRESH SAGE LEAVES
5 CLOVES GARLIC, WHOLE
¾ CUP DRY WHITE WINE
½ CUBE CHICKEN-FLAVOR STOCK
KITCHEN TWINE

Slice the turkey breast almost all the way through, and lay open. Sprinkle with a large pinch of salt and some freshly ground pepper. Arrange the slices of ham on top and lay the slices of cheese over the ham. Add the artichoke hearts, laying them in the middle. Remove and discard the sausage casing and break up the sausage over the cheese. Roll up the turkey breast lengthwise and tie up firmly with the kitchen twine. Coat with seasoned flour. In a large nonstick saucepan, gently heat the olive oil, add the rosemary, sage, and garlic. Sauté for 3 minutes, until the garlic is lightly colored. Remove the herbs and garlic from the pan. Add the turkey roll and brown gently on all sides. Add the wine and the sautéed garlic cloves, simmer for 10 minutes or until the liquid has reduced by half. Add ¾ cup of water and the stock cube half. Cover the pan. Simmer gently for at least 1 hour and 30 minutes, turning the roll occasionally and stirring the sauce. At the end of the cooking time, the garlic cloves will have softened into the sauce. The sauce will have thickened with the turkey juices and flour. Remove the roll and let it cool. Slice the roll and arrange on a serving plate, spooning the sauce over the top. Serve with roasted potatoes or vegetables and rice.

VARIATION:
Instead of the artichoke and sausage filling, an effective and colorful variation is a one-egg omelet sprinkled with your favorite chopped vegetable. Cook the omelet in your smallest nonstick round skillet. Our favorite is with peas, for when the pea omelet is rolled up in the turkey breast and sliced at the end of the cooking time, it is very eye-catching and, of course, equally flavorful.

Rotolo di Vitello Farcito

VEAL ROLL FILLED WITH SPINACH AND PARMESAN CHEESE

6 servings – preparation 20 min. – cooking time 70 min.

Make an impression the next time you have company! This dish is similar to our turkey roll (pages 78–79) and equally flavorful.

¼ CUP OLIVE OIL, PLUS 1 TABLESPOON
2 EGGS, BEATEN
SALT AND BLACK PEPPER
½ TEASPOON GROUND NUTMEG
3 TABLESPOONS GRATED PARMESAN CHEESE
1 CUP COOKED SPINACH, FRESH OR FROZEN
1 (2-POUND) VEAL BREAST, OPENED FLAT
3 CLOVES GARLIC, WHOLE
⅓ CUP WHITE WINE
½ CUBE BEEF-FLAVOR STOCK (OPTIONAL)
KITCHEN TWINE

In a small round nonstick skillet, heat 1 tablespoon of olive oil. Mix the eggs with salt and pepper to taste, nutmeg, Parmesan and spinach, and pour into the pan. Cook on both sides over medium heat. When done, lay the omelet on the veal. Roll up the veal lengthwise and tie it securely with kitchen twine. Heat the remaining ¼ cup of olive oil in a nonstick saucepan, and gently sauté the garlic cloves. Remove from the pan. Add the veal roll and gently brown on all sides. Add the garlic, white wine, and salt and pepper to taste. Then add ⅓ cup of water and the stock cube half. Allow the veal to cook for 1 hour, turning and stirring occasionally, adding small amounts of water if necessary. After 1 hour, the sauce should be reduced to the consistency of gravy. If the sauce is too watery, remove the veal and reduce to the desired consistency. Preheat the oven to 350°F. Allow the veal roll to cool before slicing, otherwise the slices tend to break apart. Arrange the sliced roll on an ovenproof serving dish, spoon over the gravy, cover with aluminum foil and warm at 350°F in the oven for 10 minutes. Serve with roasted potatoes, vegetables, and salad.

Scaloppine al Limone
VEAL SCALLOPS WITH LEMON SAUCE

4 servings – preparation 35 min. – cooking time 20 min.

This dish is quick, easy to prepare, and delicately flavored.

¼ CUP OLIVE OIL
2 LEMONS
BLACK PEPPER
1 POUND THINLY SLICED VEAL SCALLOPS
SALT
3 TABLESPOONS CHOPPED FRESH PARSLEY

In a bowl, mix 1 tablespoon of the olive oil with the juice of one lemon and some freshly ground pepper to taste. Add the veal and marinate in the refrigerator for at least 30 minutes, turning occasionally. Put the remaining 3 tablespoons of olive oil in a large nonstick skillet, and over medium heat cook the veal slices on both sides, approximately 1 to 2 minutes per side. Place the veal in a heated serving dish. Add the marinade to the oil that is left in the pan, plus the juice of the second lemon. Add salt and pepper to taste. Mix well, heat the sauce and continue stirring while the sauce reduces slightly. Pour over the veal scallops and serve them sprinkled with freshly chopped parsley. Accompany with sautéed potatoes, roasted potatoes, or salad.

VARIATION:
Boneless turkey breast may be used instead of the veal, if preferred.

Pesce
FISH

In Italy, fish is lovingly prepared, and in keeping with the cuisine, entic-
ingly flavored with simple yet effective ingredients. These are selected to
compliment the flavor of the fish, not overpower it. In many dishes, the
flavor of the fish is enhanced with garlic, parsley, white wine, and chile
peppers; and, depending on the fish, other common ingredients include
rosemary, oregano, capers, olives, tomatoes, olive oil, bread crumbs and pine
nuts. For broiled or baked fish, sliced lemon is always at hand, and when
freshly caught, cooked, and eaten on the Tuscan Mediterranean seaside,
one is momentarily transported to gastronomical heaven.

One of our first holidays to the Tuscan coast was memorable for many
reasons, but we fondly recall a leisurely Sunday lunch enjoyed in the com-
pany of good friends and family at a picturesque cliffside restaurant, over-
looking the Gulf of Baratti and the castle of Populonia. As we approached,
up a long windy gravel drive, the constant whir of crickets and bird song
filled the air, along with the tantalizing aromas drifting down from the
restaurant. The staff were friendly and the meal was outstanding. As is the
custom for large groups or special occasions, the waiter made some sugges-
tions, and trusting in his expertise, we put down our menus and accepted
his advice. After which, platter after platter of various fish and seafood-
based appetizers and pasta dishes, followed by broiled fish, sauteed pota-
toes, and mixed salad arrived. Of course all of this was accompanied by a
few good bottles of white wine, and finished with a refreshing lemon sorbet.

After a morning at the beach and this meal (which lasted 4 hours), we
took a stroll around the gulf and the grounds of the castle. All in all, we
experienced what we still feel was a perfect day.

Orata al Cartoccio

SEA BASS BAKED IN FOIL

4 servings – preparation 15 min. – cooking time 1 hr.

4 BAKING POTATOES, CLEANED AND SLICED
4 (1-POUND) FRESH SEA BASS, CLEANED AND SCALED
SALT
1 LEMON, CUT INTO 8 SLICES
1 TOMATO, CUT INTO 8 SLICES
½ CUP OLIVES
½ CUP CAPERS
4 TEASPOONS DRIED OREGANO
¾ CUP OLIVE OIL

Preheat the oven to 400°F. Grease 4 squares of foil, large enough to enclose a fish and a potato. On each piece of foil, lay a sliced potato and place a sea bass on top. Sprinkle with salt. Put two slices of lemon and two of tomato into the cavity of each fish. Add a few olives and capers to each packet, and sprinkle with oregano and salt to taste. Drizzle olive oil inside and over the fish. Wrap each fish in the aluminum foil and lay in a baking dish. Bake for 1 hour. Serve with a crusty loaf of bread and a salad.

VARIATION:
Rainbow trout or halibut steaks are appropriate substitutes, if sea bass is not readily available.

Filetti di Merluzzo Fritti

FRIED COD FILLETS

4 servings – preparation 10 min. – cooking time 15 min.

Another easy midweek option that often appeals to children.

½ CUP FLOUR, OR 1 BEATEN EGG AND ½ CUP DRY BREAD CRUMBS
4 (1-POUND) COD FILLETS, FRESH OR THAWED
¼ CUP SUNFLOWER OIL
1 LEMON
SALT

The cod fillets can be coated either in flour or in egg and then bread crumbs, and fried. They are tasty either way. Heat the sunflower oil and fry the fillets until they are crisp on both sides. Lay the fish on a plate covered with paper toweling to absorb any excess oil. Then arrange on a warm serving platter. Serve immediately with a good sprinkling of salt and a nice squeeze of lemon. Serve with salad or sautéed potatoes or both!

VARIATION:
The cod can be replaced with haddock, sole, or halibut.

Filetti di Merluzzo al Pomodoro

COD FILLETS IN TOMATO SAUCE

4 servings – preparation 5 min. – cooking time 15 min.

This is extremely quick and easy to prepare for a nutritious and tasty mid-week supper.

1½ CUPS TOMATO SAUCE (PAGE 58)
4 LARGE (1-POUND) COD FILLETS, FRESH OR THAWED
12 CAPERS, DRAINED
12 GREEN OLIVES, DRAINED
SALT

Put the tomato sauce in a broad skillet that has a tight lid and heat it. Add the cod. Cover the pan and simmer for about 10 minutes. Add the capers and olives to the pan. Add salt to taste, cover and simmer for another 5 minutes. Serve with a crusty loaf of bread, so you can soak up the sauce.

Polpette di Pesce
FISH CAKES

6 servings – preparation 30 min. – cooking time 10 min.

---

1 POUND BOILING POTATOES, PEELED AND CHOPPED INTO CHUNKS
2 POUNDS COD OR HALIBUT FILLETS
$\frac{1}{4}$ CUP OLIVE OIL
1 ONION, CHOPPED
$\frac{1}{2}$ POUND SHELLED SMALL SHRIMP, COOKED
2 TABLESPOONS CHOPPED FRESH PARSLEY
SALT AND BLACK PEPPER
2 EGGS, BEATEN
$1\frac{1}{2}$ CUPS DRY BREAD CRUMBS

Boil the potatoes for 20 minutes. Drain and mash. Meanwhile, cook the fish for 10 minutes in a pot of boiling water. Drain well and flake the fillets into a large mixing bowl. Heat 1 tablespoon of the olive oil in a large nonstick skillet and sauté the onion until it is translucent. After 5 minutes, add the shrimp and cook gently for another 5 minutes. Add the onion and shrimp to the fish, and mix well. Add the parsley, potatoes, and salt and pepper to taste. Bind all the ingredients together with the beaten eggs. If the mixture is too runny to make into fish cakes, add bread crumbs until it is firm enough to mold. Shape the mixture into 20 balls (each the size of a small lemon), and then squash slightly. Roll the fish cakes in bread crumbs. Heat the 3 remaining tablespoons of olive oil and sauté until golden brown. Serve with a salad and sautéed potatoes.

Cacciucco

FISH SOUP

6 servings – preparation 15 min. – cooking time 30 min.

This soup is excellent served with slices of toasted bread. You may also serve it over rice or tossed with spaghetti. It is versatile, and easily prepared. Fresh fish is best but frozen is a suitable substitute.

3 TABLESPOONS OLIVE OIL
4 CLOVES GARLIC, FINELY CHOPPED
3 TABLESPOONS CHOPPED FRESH PARSLEY
1 POUND SQUID RINGS
¾ CUP DRY WHITE WINE
1 (8-OUNCE) CAN PLUM TOMATOES
1 POUND COD FILLETS, SLICED
1 POUND SHRIMP, PEELED
1 TEASPOON GROUND RED HOT CHILES

In a large nonstick saucepan, or even more suitable, a nonstick wok, heat the olive oil and gently sauté the garlic and parsley. Add the squid rings to the pan and mix well. Add the white wine, cover, and simmer for 40 minutes, stirring occasionally. If the wine evaporates before the end of the cooking time, add ½ cup of water. Chop the canned tomatoes and add to the pan with their juice. Add the fish, shrimp, and chiles. Stir well and cook uncovered over medium heat for another 15 minutes.

VARIATION:
Shellfish, such as mussels and clams (approximately 1 dozen of each), make a full-flavored addition: Remove any cracked or open shells. Wash and scrub the shellfish carefully. When they are clean, put them in a bowl and cover them with water. Drain the water at least three times, to avoid adding sand to your soup. Cook them apart from the rest of the fish. Place them in a pot with 1 cup of water, cover, and steam over high heat. When the shells open, drain and remove from the pot. Once cooled, remove the fish from the shells and set aside. Discard any unopened shells. Stir the shellfish into the soup at the end of the cooking time and serve immediately.

Palombo alla Livornese

HAKE, LIVORNO STYLE

6 servings – preparation 25 min. – cooking time 40 min.

¼ CUP OLIVE OIL
1 ONION, FINELY CHOPPED
1 CARROT, PEELED AND FINELY CHOPPED
6 (1½ POUNDS) HAKE FILLETS
1 CUP FLOUR
SALT AND PEPPER
¾ CUP WHITE WINE
5 FRESH OR CANNED PLUM TOMATOES, CHOPPED

Heat the olive oil in a large nonstick pan, and gently sauté the vegetables for 10 minutes. Lightly flour the fish and add to the pan. Cook for 5 minutes on each side. Add salt and pepper to taste, and the wine. When the wine has completely reduced, add the tomatoes. Cover the pan and simmer gently for 30 minutes.

VARIATION:
This recipe also works well with swordfish, cod, haddock, or halibut.

Rombo con Salsa di Limone e Prezzemolo

HALIBUT FILLETS WITH LEMON SAUCE

6 servings – preparation 10 min. – cooking time 15 min.

This fish is divine brushed with our lemon sauce and served with rice. Children enjoy the fillets with sautéed potatoes, and ketchup or tartar sauce for dipping.

$\frac{1}{2}$ CUP SESAME SEEDS
1 CUP DRY BREAD CRUMBS
1 EGG, BEATEN
6 ($1\frac{1}{2}$-POUNDS) HALIBUT OR HAKE FILLETS
SALT
$\frac{1}{4}$ CUP OLIVE OIL
LEMON SAUCE (PAGE 54)

On a large plate, combine the sesame seeds and bread crumbs. Dip the fillets in the beaten egg and then roll them in the crumb mixture. Sprinkle each fillet with salt. In a large, nonstick skillet, heat the olive oil. Fry the fish on both sides until well browned. Lay the fish on a plate covered with paper toweling to absorb any excess oil. Then place on a warm platter. Drizzle with the Lemon Sauce.

Salmone al Forno

BAKED SALMON

6 servings – preparation 10 min. – cooking time 1 hr.

Although this is not a traditional Tuscan dish, it has become popular in our region. In Tuscany, many families welcome the New Year with this dish. It is a classic, enjoyed the world over.

1 (3-POUND) WHOLE FRESH SALMON, CLEANED AND SCALED
2 SPRIGS FRESH ROSEMARY
2 LEMONS, SLICED
SALT
5 TABLESPOONS OLIVE OIL

Preheat the oven to 375°F. Lay the salmon on aluminum foil and place the lemon slices and rosemary in the cavity. Sprinkle lightly with salt inside and out. Drizzle with olive oil inside and out. Bake, uncovered, for 1 hour. The salmon is cooked to perfection when it flakes easily off the bone. Serve with rice and salad.

Gamberoni Stuzzicanti

SPICY JUMBO SHRIMP

4 servings – preparation 10 min. – cooking time 10 min.

2 TABLESPOONS OLIVE OIL
3 CLOVES GARLIC, FINELY CHOPPED
½ TEASPOON GROUND RED HOT CHILES OR CHILE POWDER
3 TABLESPOONS CHOPPED FRESH PARSLEY
16 JUMBO SHRIMP
½ CUP DRY WHITE WINE
SALT

Heat the olive oil in a nonstick saucepan, and sauté the garlic. Add the chile and parsley. Stir in the shrimp and pour the white wine into the pan. Sprinkle with a touch of salt. Turn up the heat to high and cook uncovered for 5 minutes. Lay the shrimp side by side on a warm serving plate and reduce by half the remaining pan juices. Pour the sauce over the shrimp. Serve with toasted crusty bread rounds or rice.

VARIATIONS:
Scallops may be used as a substitute for, or included with, the shrimp (1 pound or ½ pound of each). Squid rings are also ideal. The method for the squid is the same, but it must simmer in a covered pan for at least 40 minutes, or until tender. Uncover and reduce the sauce if necessary.

Half a 4-ounce can of peeled tomatoes with their juice may also be added to the sauce, if desired.

Pesce Spada

MARINATED SWORDFISH STEAKS

4 servings – preparation 10 min. – cooking time 15 min.

This is a slightly more complicated way of cooking swordfish, but well worth the extra effort. The preparation and cooking time is short; the only thing you need to prepare in advance is the marinade, as the fish needs to soak in it for two hours. As swordfish is quite expensive, it is a nice dish to do on a Sunday or for a special occasion. We prefer an outdoor barbecue on a lazy summer afternoon, which makes it taste even better still!

$3/4$ CUP OLIVE OIL
JUICE OF 3 LEMONS
1 CLOVE GARLIC, CRUSHED
2 SPRIGS FRESH ROSEMARY
SALT
4 ($1\frac{1}{2}$-POUNDS) SWORDFISH STEAKS, FRESH OR THAWED

Combine the olive oil, lemon juice, garlic, rosemary and salt to taste, making a marinade. Reserve $1/4$ cup of the marinade in a separate bowl, to use later as a sauce. Lay the fish in a pan and pour the remaining marinade over it. Place the reserved marinade and the marinated fish in the fridge for 2 hours.

For best results, a hot charcoal grill or barbecue is required. Place the swordfish on the grill over the hot coals and cook on each side for about 10 minutes. While it cooks, baste continuously with the marinade, using an extra-long sprig of rosemary or a heatproof brush. Serve each fish topped with 2 tablespoons of the reserved marinade.

VARIATION:
Halibut steaks are a suitable substitute for the swordfish steaks.

Pesce Spada al Forno

OVEN-BAKED SWORDFISH STEAKS

6 servings – preparation 10 min. – cooking time 30 min.

---

3 CLOVES GARLIC, FINELY CHOPPED
3 TABLESPOONS CHOPPED FRESH PARSLEY
1 TEASPOON DRIED OREGANO
6 (1½-POUNDS) SWORDFISH STEAKS, SKIN REMOVED
SALT AND BLACK PEPPER
⅓ CUP OLIVE OIL
¾ CUP DRY WHITE WINE
3 TABLESPOONS CAPERS

Preheat the oven to 375°F. Mix the garlic with the parsley and oregano. Sprinkle salt and pepper over the fish to taste and roll in the garlic mixture. Grease a pan large enough to hold all the fish in a single layer and add the fish. Sprinkle the remaining garlic mixture over them. Add the white wine and sprinkle the fish with the capers. Bake for 30 minutes. Serve with bread and salad.

VARIATION:

Halibut steaks are a suitable substitute for the swordfish steaks.

Pesce Spada alla Griglia
PANFRIED SWORDFISH STEAKS

4 servings – preparation 5 min. – cooking time 20 min.

¼ CUP OLIVE OIL
4 (1½-POUNDS) SWORDFISH STEAKS, FRESH OR THAWED
1 LEMON
SALT

Heat the olive oil in a skillet and add the swordfish steaks. Cook on each side for about 5 to 10 minutes. When cooked, add a squeeze of lemon and salt to taste. To serve, cover the steak with pan juices and extra lemon juice, if desired.

VARIATION:
Halibut steaks are a suitable substitute for the swordfish steaks.

Pizza e Pasta Sfoglia
PIZZAS AND PIES

In Tuscany, pizza is cooked in dome-shaped, wood-fired ovens, which are a typical feature in many restaurants. Pizza is the perfect solution for dinner and birthday parties, and enjoyed by young and old alike. It is also a wonderful romantic meal to share.

In true Italian fashion, Madeline's husband, Mimmo, likes to celebrate Valentine's day by serving heart-shaped pizza to his beloved. The Nocentini family enjoy pizza cooked in their wood-fired oven. Their "pizza nights" take place in the height of summer outside on their garden terrace. They set a table for twenty or more under the grapevines, and the whole family shares in the preparation and cooking. Many friends have been enchanted by the food, atmosphere, and a glass or two of Giovanni's homemade Grappa.

After years of enjoying traditional Italian pizza, we have created the following list, which is based on the most popular pizzas served in Italian homes and restaurants. Prior to making our selection, we spoke with our friend, Antonio Tacconi, owner of I'Tacca, Pizzeria e Ristorante, and he kindly shared his preferences. This list should serve as a basic guide. Be inspired and let your creativity loose.

We also have the pleasure of sharing three special recipes. Diane's sister-in-law, Paola Nocentini, has provided her tomato sauce recipe that, in its simplicity, is the perfect base for a delicious pizza. Our friend, Enrica Palermo, has shared her pizza dough recipe. Enrica is from Sicily and, needless to say, a reliable source for the perfect crust. Diane's mother-in-law, Maria Nocentini, has also blessed us with her dough recipe, which the family testifies is the best.

Italian pizza is served, according to preference, with or without tomato sauce, and unless otherwise specified, mozzarella is used.

CLASSIC ITALIAN PIZZA TOPPINGS

Capricciosa	Italian sausage and artichoke
Due Stagioni	Two Seasons: Italian sausage and onion
Estiva	Summertime: fresh tomatoes, basil, garlic, and oregano
Gorgonzola and Rucola	Italian blue cheese and arugula
Margherita	Tomato sauce and mozzarella
Melanzane and Peperoni	Roasted eggplant and red/yellow bell peppers
Napoli	Neapolitan: anchovies and capers
Porcini	Porcini mushrooms
Prosciutto and Funghi	Cooked ham and mushrooms
Quattro Formaggi	Four Cheese: mozzarella, fontina, Gorgonzola, and pecorino or provolone
Quattro Stagioni	Four Seasons: artichoke, hot dog, ham, mushrooms and olives, grouped into four sections
Schiacciata	A simple Tuscan flatbread, seasoned with salt and oregano, to serve with *Tegamino* (page 101), or covered with Parma ham, arugula, and shavings of Parmesan
Speck and Provolone	Smoked ham and provolone
Tonno and Cipolla	Canned tuna with onions: sauté the onions with olive oil, salt, and oregano, prior to topping your pizza
Vegetariana	Vegetarian: roasted eggplant, zucchini, bell peppers, and seasoned spinach

L'impasto di Enrica
ENRICA'S PIZZA DOUGH

8 servings – prep. 20 min. – resting time 4 hr. – cooking time 20 min.

This produces a thick crust.

---

1 (1-TABLESPOON) PACKET ACTIVE DRY YEAST
1¾ CUPS WARM WATER
7 CUPS ALL-PURPOSE FLOUR
1 SMALL BOILING POTATO, BOILED AND MASHED
2 TABLESPOONS SALT
⅓ CUP OLIVE OIL

Dissolve the yeast in the warm water. On a work surface, combine the flour, potato, and salt. Form a mound with a well or deep indentation in the middle. Gradually add the yeast mixture and then the olive oil to the well. Knead the dough until a uniform ball is formed (10 minutes). The dough is the correct consistency when it stops sticking to your fingers. Sprinkle with more flour if needed. Enrica says the dough should feel like your ear lobe and, when you push a finger in, it will spring back, filling half the hole. Oil your hands and roll the ball of dough, coating it thinly with oil. This prevents a dry crust from forming. Put the dough in a large mixing bowl and cover the bowl with a warm, damp tea towel. Leave it to rise for 4 hours. The dough must be kept warm. Enrica even suggests wrapping a blanket around the bowl. The dough should be doubled in size in this time. Preheat oven to 500°F. Lightly oil three pizza pans (12-inch diameter). Divide the dough into three balls and stretch them onto the pans with your hands. Top as desired and bake at 500°F for approximately 15 to 20 minutes. At this point the dough should be browned underneath, and the top bubbling and lightly colored.

L'impasto di Maria

MARIA'S PIZZA DOUGH

4 servings – prep. 20 min. – resting time 4 hr. – cooking time 20 min.

This makes a thin crust.

3½ CUPS ALL-PURPOSE FLOUR
1 CUP WARM WATER
1 TABLESPOON SALT
1 TABLESPOON SUGAR
¾ CUP CORN OIL
½ PACKET (½ TABLESPOON) ACTIVE DRY YEAST

The method is the same as in Enrica's recipe (page 99) except that the potato is omitted. When the dough has risen, divide into two balls, and without creating holes, stretch the dough as thinly as possible onto two lightly oiled pans (12-inch diameter).

La Salsa di Paola

PAOLA'S TOMATO SAUCE FOR PIZZA

---

3 CUPS TOMATO SAUCE (PAGE 58)
3 TABLESPOONS OLIVE OIL
4 TABLESPOONS CHOPPED FRESH BASIL
3 TABLESPOONS DRIED OREGANO
SALT AND BLACK PEPPER TO TASTE
2 FINELY CHOPPED GARLIC CLOVES, IF DESIRED

In a nonstick sauce pan, mix all of the ingredients and simmer gently for ten minutes. Stir occasionally.

VARIATION:

Tegamino (Pizza Hot Pot): In individual crock pots, mix Paola's tomato sauce with your favorite toppings. Cover with diced mozzarella and bake at 500°F for about 10 to 15 minutes, until the cheese is golden and the mix is bubbling. Serve with plain *schiacciata* (a Tuscan flatbread) or a fresh crusty loaf for dipping.

Broccoli e Formaggio in Pasta Sfoglia
BROCCOLI AND CHEESE PUFF PASTRY PIE

6 servings – preparation 30 min. – cooking time 30 min.

1 HEAD BROCCOLI, CHOPPED
1 POUND (2 ROLLS) FROZEN PUFF PASTRY, THAWED
4 TABLESPOONS GRATED PARMESAN CHEESE
1 CUP GRATED BEL PAESE CHEESE
1 CUP HEAVY CREAM
SALT AND BLACK PEPPER
MILK OR A BEATEN EGG
2 TABLESPOONS SESAME SEEDS

Preheat the oven to 400°F. Steam the broccoli until tender. If you prefer a pressure cooker, pour in 1 cup of water and cook for 10 minutes, from the time it starts whistling. Lay one sheet of pastry flat on a nonstick baking sheet, and leaving a (1-inch) margin along the edge of the pastry for crimping, distribute the chopped broccoli over the top. Sprinkle with the Parmesan and Bel Paese cheese. Spoon on the cream and add a sprinkling of salt and pepper to taste. Lay the other pastry roll over the top and crimp the edges together with a fork. With the fork, prick holes in the top of the pastry. Brush with a little milk or a beaten egg. Sprinkle with sesame seeds and bake for 30 minutes.

Prosciutto e Mozzarella in Pasta Sfoglia
HAM AND MOZZARELLA PUFF PASTRY PIE

6 servings – preparation 12 min. – cooking time 30 min.

This is a quick recipe that often appeals to children who are reluctant eaters.

---

1 POUND (2 ROLLS) FROZEN PUFF PASTRY, THAWED
1 (8-OUNCE) PACKAGE MOZZARELLA, SLICED
1 LARGE BOILING POTATO, BOILED AND SLICED
1½ CUPS CHOPPED COOKED HAM
¾ CUP RICOTTA CHEESE
SALT AND BLACK PEPPER
MILK OR A BEATEN EGG
2 TABLESPOONS SESAME SEEDS

Preheat the oven to 400°F. Lay one sheet of pastry flat on a nonstick baking sheet, and leaving a 1-inch margin along the edge of the pastry for crimping, layer on the mozzarella, potato, ham, and ricotta. Add a sprinkling of salt and pepper to taste. Lay the other roll of pastry over the top and crimp the edges with a fork. With the fork, prick holes in the top. Brush with a little milk or beaten egg. Sprinkle with sesame seeds and bake for 30 minutes.

VARIATION:
This pie is also popular when we transform it into pizza pie. Top the pie with cooked ham, mozzarella, a little tomato sauce, and a sprinkling of oregano.

Spinaci e Ricotta in Pasta Sfoglia
SPINACH AND RICOTTA PUFF PASTRY PIE

6 servings – preparation 20 min. – cooking time 30 min.

We make this one for our children. They love "Popeye Pie."

---

1 TABLESPOON OLIVE OIL
1 SMALL ONION, CHOPPED
3 CUPS COOKED SPINACH
2 TEASPOONS GROUND NUTMEG
SALT AND BLACK PEPPER
3 CUPS RICOTTA CHEESE
1 POUND (2 ROLLS) FROZEN PUFF PASTRY, THAWED
MILK OR A BEATEN EGG
2 TABLESPOONS SESAME SEEDS

Preheat the oven to 400°F. Heat the olive oil and sauté the onion for 3 minutes, until translucent. Add the cooked spinach and nutmeg. Stir in salt and pepper to taste. Cool. Mix the ricotta with the cooled spinach mixture. Lay one roll of the puff pastry flat on a nonstick baking sheet, and leaving a 1-inch margin along the edge of the pastry for crimping, spread the spinach mixture over the top. Lay the other roll of pastry over the top and crimp the edges with a fork. With the fork, prick holes in the top, and brush with a little milk or beaten egg. Sprinkle with sesame seeds and bake for 30 minutes.

VARIATION:

This pie is also scrumptious if you sauté two or three finely chopped cloves of garlic (instead of the onion) in the olive oil. Add the spinach and 4 slices of chopped cooked ham or bacon. Add ½ cup of tomato sauce and ¾ cup of grated Parmesan cheese, instead of the ricotta. Mix well. The rest of the method is the same.

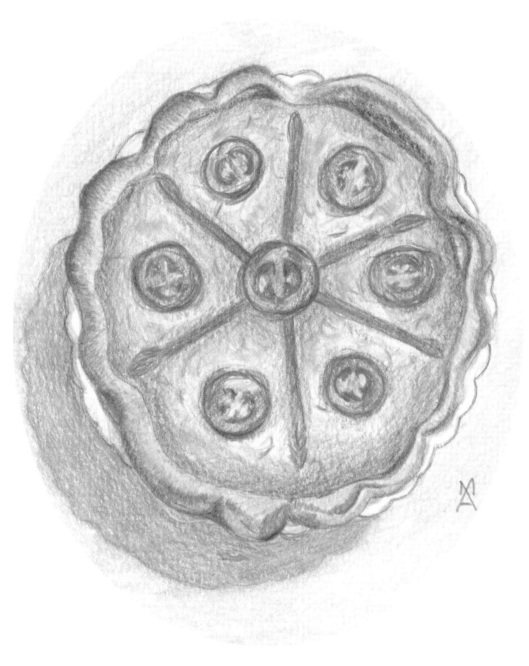

Quiche

QUICHE

As quiche is becoming popular in Tuscany, we decided to include a small selection. Homemade quiche is much better than the bought variety. It is not difficult to make and is well worth the effort. If you use a readymade shortcrust pastry, your job will be even easier. Served with a salad, quiche makes a lovely light lunch or supper to share with friends or family. We have included our favorite recipes, which are truly a triumph of flavor.

Pasta Brisé

SHORTCRUST PASTRY

preparation 15 min. – resting time 30 min.

This recipe makes enough pastry to line an 11-inch diameter flan pan.

1⅔ CUPS ALL-PURPOSE FLOUR
A PINCH OF SALT
⅓ CUP BUTTER
⅓ CUP MARGARINE OR SHORTENING
2 TABLESPOONS COLD WATER

Sift the flour and salt into a mixing bowl, and rub in the butter and margarine until the mixture resembles bread crumbs. Add the cold water and mix the pastry into a ball. Allow the pastry to rest for 30 minutes at room temperature. Flour a flat surface and roll the pastry out until it is the size of the flan pan.

Quiche con Porri e Speck

LEEK AND SMOKED HAM QUICHE

6 servings – preparation 30 min. – cooking time 40 min.

SHORTCRUST PASTRY (PAGE 106)
2 TABLESPOONS OLIVE OIL
2 LEEKS, WASHED AND SLICED INTO RINGS
$1\frac{1}{2}$ CUPS CHOPPED SMOKED HAM
3 EGGS, BEATEN
$\frac{3}{4}$ CUP HEAVY CREAM
SALT AND BLACK PEPPER
1 PLUM TOMATO, THINLY SLICED
$\frac{1}{4}$ CUP GRATED PROVOLONE CHEESE

Preheat the oven to 400°F. Lay the pastry into a flan pan and prick the bottom with a fork. Bake for 15 minutes. Heat the olive oil in a nonstick skillet and gently sauté the leeks until soft. In a mixing bowl, combine the leeks, ham, eggs, and cream. Add salt and pepper to taste. Place the leek mixture into the pastry, and arrange the tomato slices on top. Sprinkle with the grated cheese. Bake for 40 minutes, or until the filling is firm and the top is golden brown.

Quiche con Zucchini e Gamberi

SHRIMP AND ZUCCHINI QUICHE

6 servings – preparation 30 min. – cooking time 40 min.

SHORTCRUST PASTRY (PAGE 106)
2 TABLESPOONS OLIVE OIL
1 ONION, CHOPPED
4 ZUCCHINI, THINLY SLICED
1½ CUPS COOKED, PEELED SHRIMP
SALT AND BLACK PEPPER
¾ CUP HEAVY CREAM
3 EGGS
¼ CUP GRATED BEL PAESE CHEESE

Preheat the oven to 400°F. Lay the pastry into a flan pan and prick the bottom with a fork. Bake for 15 minutes. Heat the olive oil in a nonstick skillet and sauté the onion and zucchini for 10 minutes, or until golden. Stir in the shrimp and sauté for another 5 minutes, until heated. Add salt and pepper to taste. In a large bowl, mix the cream, eggs, and half the cheese. Add the shrimp mixture. Mix well and place into the flan crust. Sprinkle the rest of the grated cheese on top and bake for 40 minutes, or until the filling is firm and the top is golden brown. Serve with salad and crusty bread.

Quiche al Tonno
TUNA QUICHE

6 servings – preparation 30 min. – cooking time 40 min.

SHORTCRUST PASTRY (PAGE 106)
1 (10-OUNCE) CAN TUNA PACKED IN OLIVE OIL
2 WHITE ONIONS, ONE CHOPPED AND THE OTHER THINLY SLICED
¾ CUP HEAVY CREAM
3 EGGS
SALT AND BLACK PEPPER
1 PLUM TOMATO, THINLY SLICED
DRIED OREGANO

Preheat the oven to 400°F. Lay the pastry into a flan pan and prick the bottom with a fork. Bake for 15 minutes. Drain the oil from the tuna into a skillet over medium heat and sauté the chopped onion until soft. In a large bowl mix the cream, eggs, tuna, and sautéed onion. Add salt and pepper to taste and mix well. Remove the pastry from the oven and fill the crust with the tuna mixture. Arrange the onion and tomato slices decoratively on top of the quiche. Add a sprinkling of salt and oregano. Place in the oven and bake for 40 minutes, or until the filling is firm and the top is golden brown.

Crespelle Saporite
SAVORY CRÊPES

Crêpes are very popular in Italy, and extremely versatile. As a special Sunday dish, they are hard to beat, and usually appeal to everyone. We have suggested some classic fillings but basically you can fill them with anything that catches your fancy. Once covered with the béchamel sauce and baked in the oven, they always turn out wonderfully.

Crêpes freeze very well, so if you haven't got much time they can be made beforehand and frozen. Just pile them up with a sheet of waxed paper between each one and freeze. Otherwise they can always be made the day before, and when cool, piled up and stored in the fridge.

All of the following recipes are based on filling a dozen crêpes. They are sufficient for serving a party of six.

Some of our crêpe recipes include Tomato Sauce (page 58), and they all require a double recipe of Béchamel Sauce (page 54). Prepare the sauces before you start.

Crespelle
BASIC CRÊPES

6 servings (12 crêpes) – prep. 5 min. – rest 1 hr. – cooking time 30 min.

¾ CUP ALL-PURPOSE FLOUR
1 CUP WHOLE MILK
3 EGGS
1 TEASPOON SALT
1 TEASPOON BLACK PEPPER
⅓ CUP BUTTER

Beat together all of the ingredients, except for the butter. Heat a small nonstick skillet over medium-high heat and swirl with 1 teaspoon of butter. Pour in enough batter to thinly coat the pan, using once again a swirling technique to spread the batter evenly. Once bubbles start to break through the surface, check that the underside has browned and flip and cook until browned on the other side. Repeat the procedure with the remaining batter and butter.

Crespelle con Salmone e Brie
SALMON AND BRIE CRÊPES

6 servings (12 crêpes) – prep. 25 min. – cooking time 20 min.

BASIC CRÊPES RECIPE (ABOVE)
DOUBLE RECIPE BÉCHAMEL SAUCE (PAGE 54), COOLED
1 (8-OUNCE) PACKAGE SMOKED SALMON, THINLY SLICED
1½ POUNDS BRIE, THINLY SLICED
6 TABLESPOONS CHOPPED FRESH CHIVES

Make the crêpes and béchamel sauce. Preheat the oven to 400°F. On a flat surface, place on each crêpe a slice of smoked salmon, a slice of

Brie, and sprinkling of chives. Roll up each crêpe evenly. Spread a cup of the béchamel sauce in a baking pan. Place each crêpe side by side in the pan on top of the sauce. Cover with the remaining béchamel sauce and sprinkle with Parmesan. Bake for 30 minutes, until the top is golden brown.

Crespelle al Prosciutto Cotto e Mozzarella

COOKED HAM AND MOZZARELLA CRÊPES

6 servings (12 crêpes) – prep. 35 min. – cooking time 20 min.

BASIC CRÊPES RECIPE (PAGE 112)
DOUBLE RECIPE BÉCHAMEL SAUCE (PAGE 54), COOLED
1 CUP TOMATO SAUCE (PAGE 58)
12 OUNCES COOKED HAM, DICED
2 (8-OUNCE) PACKAGES MOZZARELLA, DICED
SALT AND BLACK PEPPER
5 TABLESPOONS GRATED PARMESAN CHEESE

Make the crêpes, béchamel sauce and tomato sauce. Preheat the oven to 400°F. Mix the ham, mozzarella, and 1 cup of the cooled béchamel sauce together. Add salt and pepper to taste. Spread half a cup of tomato sauce in the bottom of a baking pan (14 x 10-inch). On a flat surface, fill each crêpe with a third cup of the ham mixture. Roll up each crêpe evenly and place them side by side on top of the sauce. Cover them with the remaining béchamel sauce and spoon the rest of the tomato sauce over the top. Sprinkle with the freshly grated Parmesan. Bake for 20 minutes, until the top is golden brown.

Crespelle ai Funghi
MUSHROOM CRÊPES

6 servings (12 crêpes) – prep. 35 min. – cooking time 20 min.

If they are available, we highly recommend fresh porcini mushrooms for this recipe. Their distinct flavor is absolutely divine in crêpes.

BASIC CRÊPES RECIPE (PAGE 112)
DOUBLE RECIPE BÉCHAMEL SAUCE (PAGE 54), COOLED
1 CUP TOMATO SAUCE (PAGE 58)
3 TABLESPOONS OLIVE OIL
3 CLOVES GARLIC, CHOPPED
1½ POUNDS FRESH PORCINI OR BUTTON MUSHROOMS, FINELY
    SLICED
SALT AND BLACK PEPPER
5 TABLESPOONS GRATED PARMESAN CHEESE

Make the crêpes, béchamel sauce and tomato sauce. Preheat the oven to 400°F. Heat the olive oil in a large nonstick skillet and lightly sauté the garlic. Add the mushrooms and sauté for 15 minutes or until the mushrooms are soft. Add salt and pepper to taste. Remove from heat and mix in 1 cup of the béchamel sauce. Spread half a cup of the tomato sauce in the bottom of a baking pan. On a flat surface, fill each crêpe with a third cup of the mushroom mixture. Roll up each crêpe evenly and lay them side by side on top of the sauce. Cover with the remaining béchamel sauce and spoon the rest of the tomato sauce over the top. Sprinkle with the Parmesan. Bake for 20 minutes, until the top is golden brown.

Crespelle al Tonno
TUNA CRÊPES

6 servings (12 crêpes) – prep. 35 min. – cooking time 20 min.

DOUBLE RECIPE BÉCHAMEL SAUCE (PAGE 54), COOLED
BASIC CRÊPES RECIPE (PAGE 112)
1 CUP TOMATO SAUCE (PAGE 58)
2 (12-OUNCE) CANS TUNA, PACKED IN OLIVE OIL, DRAINED AND
    FINELY CHOPPED
3 TABLESPOONS CAPERS, FINELY CHOPPED
1 (8-OUNCE) PACKAGE MOZZARELLA, DICED
3 TABLESPOONS CHOPPED FRESH PARSLEY
1 TABLESPOON CHOPPED FRESH BASIL
SALT AND BLACK PEPPER

Make the béchamel sauce, crêpes and tomato sauce. Preheat the oven to 400°F. Combine the tuna, capers, mozzarella, parsley, basil, and salt and pepper to taste. Mix with 1 cup of béchamel sauce. In a medium-size nonstick baking pan (14 x 10-inch), spread half a cup of the tomato sauce on the bottom. On a flat surface, fill each crêpe with a third cup of the tuna mixture and roll up each crêpe evenly. Place each crêpe side by side in the pan and cover them with the béchamel sauce. Dot with the remaining tomato sauce. Bake for 30 minutes, until the top is golden brown.

Crespelle ai Frutti di Mare

SEAFOOD CRÊPES

6 servings (12 crêpes) – prep. 40 min. – cooking time 20 min.

BASIC CRÊPES RECIPE (PAGE 112)
DOUBLE RECIPE BÉCHAMEL SAUCE (PAGE 54), COOLED
2 TABLESPOONS OLIVE OIL
1 SMALL WHITE ONION, FINELY CHOPPED
2 TABLESPOONS CHOPPED FRESH PARSLEY
1 (4-OUNCE) SALMON FILLET, FINELY DICED
1 (8-OUNCE) COD FILLET, FINELY DICED
1 (8-OUNCE) PACKAGE COOKED SHRIMP
$\frac{1}{2}$ CUP DRY WHITE WINE
SALT AND BLACK PEPPER
$\frac{1}{2}$ CUP HEAVY CREAM

Make the crêpes and béchamel sauce. Preheat the oven to 400°F. Heat the olive oil in a large nonstick saucepan, and sauté the onion and parsley. Add the salmon, cod, and shrimp. Stir well and sauté for 5 minutes. Pour in the white wine and cook for 5 minutes over high heat, or until the wine evaporates. Add salt and pepper to taste. Stir in the cream. Spread a cup of the béchamel sauce in a baking pan. On a flat surface, fill each crêpe with a third cup of the seafood mixture. Roll them up evenly and place each crêpe side by side in the pan on top of the sauce. Cover them with the remaining béchamel sauce. Bake for 20 minutes, until the top is golden brown.

Crespelle con Ricotta e Spinaci
SPINACH AND RICOTTA CRÊPES

6 servings (12 crêpes) – prep. 30 min. – cooking time 30 min.

Spinach and ricotta crêpes are a classic Florentine dish. They are served in numerous restaurants and often baked for special occasions by Florentine families. Once you have tasted them, you'll know why!

BASIC CRÊPES RECIPE (PAGE 112)
DOUBLE RECIPE BÉCHAMEL SAUCE (PAGE 54), COOLED
1 CUP TOMATO SAUCE (PAGE 58)
2 TABLESPOONS OLIVE OIL
2 CLOVES GARLIC, CHOPPED
2 CUPS COOKED SPINACH
SALT AND BLACK PEPPER
1 TABLESPOON GROUND NUTMEG
2 CUPS RICOTTA CHEESE
1 BEATEN EGG
PARMESAN CHEESE, GRATED

Make the crêpes, béchamel sauce and tomato sauce. Preheat the oven to 400°F. In a large nonstick saucepan, heat the oil and sauté the garlic. Stir in the spinach. Add salt, pepper, and nutmeg to taste. Stir well and simmer for 10 minutes. Allow the mixture to cool, and then stir in the ricotta cheese and the egg. In a medium-size nonstick baking pan (14 x 10-inch), spread half a cup of the tomato sauce on the bottom. On a flat surface, fill each crêpe with a third cup of the spinach mixture and roll up each crêpe evenly. Place each crêpe side by side in the pan and cover them with the béchamel sauce. Dot with the remaining tomato sauce and then sprinkle generously with the Parmesan. Bake for 30 minutes, until the top is golden brown.

VARIATION:
Grated Parmesan cheese (1 cup) may be substituted for the ricotta, and you may enjoy adding 1 cup of diced cooked ham to the mixture. Either way, these crêpes are mouthwatering.

Uova

EGGS

Omelets (frittate) are one of our favorite things to cook. They are easy, versatile, quick, and ideal for a lunch or a weekday supper. They are also extremely useful for using up leftovers, from pasta to vegetable dishes. They are suitable for vegetarians and often appeal to children who are reluctant eaters (not always, though!).

A useful tip when making an omelet is to cook the top side under a hot broiler, avoiding all the fuss of turning it over on a plate or balancing it on a spatula and trying to flip it.

Frittata alle Melanzane

EGGPLANT OMELET

4 servings – preparation 5 min. – cooking time 15 min.

¼ CUP OLIVE OIL
1 EGGPLANT, THINLY SLICED LENGTHWISE
8 EGGS, BEATEN
SALT AND BLACK PEPPER

Preheat the broiler to 400°F. Heat the olive oil in a large nonstick oven-proof skillet, over medium heat. Sauté the eggplant slices until they are golden on both sides. Remove from the pan. Season the eggs with salt and pepper, pour into the same skillet, and lay the eggplant slices evenly over the top. Lower the heat slightly and cook the underside for 10 minutes, or until golden. Place the skillet under the broiler for 5 minutes, cooking the top until golden. Serve with salad and crusty bread.

Frittata di Pasta

PASTA OMELET

4 servings – preparation 5 min. – cooking time 15 min.

This is an original way of using up leftover pasta. We prefer using short pasta, such as penne, that has been tossed in meat or tomato sauce. As the pasta has been prepared the day before, the flavor of the sauce intensifies, giving the omelet a satisfying full flavor.

---

8 EGGS, BEATEN
2 CUPS LEFTOVER PASTA
SALT AND BLACK PEPPER
6 OUNCES FONTINA CHEESE, GRATED
2 TABLESPOONS OLIVE OIL

Heat the broiler to 400°F. Combine the eggs and the leftover pasta. Add salt and pepper to taste, and the grated cheese. Heat the olive oil in a large nonstick heatproof skillet over medium heat, and pour in the egg mixture. Lower the heat slightly and cook for 10 minutes, until the underside is golden. Place the skillet under the broiler, and cook the top of the omelet for 5 minutes, or until golden. Serve with salad and crusty bread.

Frittata di Patate e Verdure
POTATO AND VEGETABLE OMELET

4 servings – preparation 5 min. – cooking time 15 min.

8 EGGS, BEATEN
4 POTATOES, BOILED OR ROASTED, DICED
1 CUP VEGETABLES, BOILED OR ROASTED, DICED
6 OUNCES PECORINO CHEESE, GRATED
SALT AND BLACK PEPPER
2 TABLESPOONS OLIVE OIL

Heat the broiler to 400°F. Mix the eggs with the potatoes, vegetables, and cheese. Add salt and pepper to taste. Heat the oil in a large nonstick ovenproof skillet over medium heat and pour in the egg mixture. Lower the heat slightly and cook the underside slowly for 10 minutes, or until golden. Place the skillet under the broiler, and cook the top of the omelet for 5 minutes or until golden. Serve with salad and crusty bread.

VARIATION:
Broccoli, zucchini, and spinach are all good substitutes for the potatoes, but remember satisfy personal tastes, be adventurous, and use up those leftovers.

Uova al Pancetta e Cipolla

POACHED EGGS WITH BACON BITS AND ONION

4 servings – preparation 10 min. – cooking time 10 min.

2 TABLESPOONS OLIVE OIL
½ ONION, FINELY CHOPPED
5 SLICES BACON, COOKED AND DICED
2½ CUPS TOMATO SAUCE (PAGE 58)
SALT AND BLACK PEPPER
8 EGGS

Heat the olive oil in a 10-inch diameter nonstick saucepan, and sauté the onion until soft. Add the bacon, tomato sauce, and salt and pepper to taste. Over medium heat, bring the sauce to a slow boil, crack the eggs over the sauce, being careful not to break the eggs. Sprinkle a little salt on each egg. Cover the pan and lower the heat. Cook for 10 minutes, or until the eggs are firm.

Uova al Prosciutto e Piselli

POACHED EGGS WITH PEAS AND HAM

4 servings – preparation 5 min. – cooking time 10 min.

SINGLE RECIPE PEAS AND HAM (PAGE 140)
8 EGGS
SALT

In a 10-inch diameter nonstick skillet, over medium heat, warm the peas and ham and let them cook. Then crack the eggs on top of them, being careful not to break the eggs. Sprinkle a little salt on each egg. Cover the pan and lower the heat. Cook for 10 minutes, or until the eggs are firm.

Uova agli Spinaci

POACHED EGGS WITH SPINACH

4 servings – preparation 5 min. – cooking time 10 min.

SINGLE RECIPE SPINACH WITH GARLIC AND OIL (PAGE 145)
8 EGGS
SALT

In a 10-inch diameter nonstick skillet, over medium heat, warm the spinach, and ½ a cup of water. Crack the eggs on top, being careful not to break them. Sprinkle a little salt on each egg. Cover the pan and lower the heat. Cook for 10 minutes, or until the eggs are firm.

Uova al Pomodoro

POACHED EGGS IN TOMATO SAUCE

4 servings – preparation 5 min. – cooking time 10 min.

2½ CUPS TOMATO SAUCE (PAGE 58)
8 EGGS
SALT
DRIED OREGANO

Spread the tomato sauce in the bottom of a 10-inch diameter nonstick skillet. Over medium heat, warm the tomato sauce and crack the eggs over the sauce, being careful not to break the eggs. On each egg, sprinkle a little salt and oregano. Cover the saucepan and lower the heat. Cook gently for 10 minutes, or until the eggs are firm. Serve with crusty bread.

Uova alle Zucchine

POACHED EGGS WITH TOMATO AND BASIL ZUCCHINI

4 servings – preparation 5 min. – cooking time 10 min.

HALF RECIPE TOMATO AND BASIL ZUCCHINI (PAGE 149)
8 EGGS
SALT

In a 10-inch diameter nonstick skillet, over medium heat, warm the zucchini mixture and crack the eggs on top, being careful not to break them. Sprinkle a little salt on each egg. Cover the pan and lower the heat. Cook for 10 minutes, or until the eggs are firm.

Verdure
VEGETABLES

Italians often eat vegetables that have been either steamed or lightly boiled. They dress them simply with olive oil, lemon juice, salt, and pepper. This is a tasty and very healthy way of eating. The heat of the steamed vegetables brings out the distinct flavor of the olive oil, and the tang of the lemon juice adds just the right balance. Appropriate vegetables to cook in this way are green beans, zucchini, broccoli, and asparagus. Another way of enjoying vegetables is to steam and then sauté them in olive oil and garlic. Try spinach, beet greens, cabbage, broccoli, green beans, or any green leaf vegetable, such as kale for this method.

Involtini di Asparagini

ASPARAGUS WRAPS

8 servings – preparation 20 min. – cooking time 25 min.

---

24 THIN SPEARS FRESH ASPARAGUS
1 TEASPOON SALT
4 THIN SLICES COOKED HAM, HALVED LENGTHWISE
8 THIN SLICES FONTINA CHEESE
PARMESAN CHEESE, GRATED
⅓ CUP BUTTER

Wash, trim, and boil the asparagus in salted water for 10 minutes. Drain immediately. Preheat the oven to 400°F. Grease a 14 x 10-inch baking pan. Place three spears of asparagus together and roll a half slice of ham around them. Continue with the remaining asparagus and ham. Lay the wraps next to each other in the pan. Place a thin slice of cheese on each bundle, sprinkle them with grated Parmesan, and dot lightly with butter. Bake on the highest rack for 15 minutes, and serve.

VARIATION:
If you wish to simplify this dish, eliminate the ham and Fontina cheese. Just lay the boiled asparagus in a baking pan, dot with butter, sprinkle liberally with freshly grated Parmesan cheese, and bake as directed. *Asparagi alla parmigiana* is an old Italian favorite.

Cavolo con Pomodoro

CABBAGE AND TOMATOES

6 servings – preparation 15 min. – cooking time 45 min.

3 TABLESPOONS OLIVE OIL
½ ONION, CHOPPED
4 OR 5 FRESH OR CANNED PLUM TOMATOES, CHOPPED
3 LEAVES FRESH BASIL, CHOPPED
1 POUND SAVOY CABBAGE, CHOPPED
SALT AND BLACK PEPPER

Heat the olive oil in a nonstick lidded saucepan and sauté the onion until soft. Add the tomatoes, basil, and cabbage and sauté for 5 minutes. Add 1¾ cups of water, cover the pan, and simmer for 15 minutes, until the cabbage is tender but not mushy. Adjust the flavor with salt and pepper.

VARIATION:
This vegetable dish when served with penne, as a sauce or an accompaniment, makes a very satisfying first course. Spice it up with a drop or two of Red Hot Chile Oil (page 7).

Sformato di Cavolfiore
CAULIFLOWER BAKE

6 servings – preparation 15 min. – cooking time 40 min.

1 TABLESPOON BUTTER
1 TABLESPOON FLOUR
1 HEAD CAULIFLOWER, CUT INTO FLORETS
2 TABLESPOONS SALT (OR TO TASTE)
2 TABLESPOONS OLIVE OIL
1 ONION, FINELY CHOPPED
2 EGGS
1 CUP BÉCHAMEL SAUCE (PAGE 54)
½ CUP GRATED PARMESAN CHEESE
1½ TEASPOONS GROUND NUTMEG
SALT AND BLACK PEPPER
3 TABLESPOONS DRY BREAD CRUMBS

Preheat the oven to 400°F. Grease and flour a 10-inch diameter baking dish. Boil the cauliflower in salted water for only 10 minutes, as it will finish cooking in the oven. Drain and cool, then finely chop. Heat the olive oil in a small nonstick skillet and gently sauté the onion until translucent. In a large mixing bowl, beat the eggs with the béchamel sauce. Add half the cheese, 1 teaspoon of the nutmeg, and salt and pepper to taste. Add the cauliflower and onion, and mix well. Pour the mixture into the baking dish and sprinkle the top with the remaining Parmesan, bread crumbs, and the remaining ½ teaspoon of nutmeg. Bake for 40 minutes. At the end of the cooking time, turn on the broiler. Broil until the top is golden.

Cavolfiore in Forno
CAULIFLOWER WITH BÉCHAMEL SAUCE

4 servings – preparation 5 min. – cooking time 30 min.

---

1 HEAD CAULIFLOWER
2 TABLESPOONS SALT (OR TO TASTE)
1 TABLESPOON BUTTER
SINGLE RECIPE BÉCHAMEL SAUCE (PAGE 54)
3/4 CUP GRATED PARMESAN CHEESE
2 TEASPOONS GROUND NUTMEG

Preheat the oven to 400°F. Clean the cauliflower and remove the large leaves. Cut a cross into the stem (to ensure that the cauliflower cooks evenly), and place in a large pot of salted boiling water. Boil only for 10 minutes, as the cauliflower will finish cooking in the oven, and drain. Grease a 12 x 9-inch baking dish with butter. Cut the cauliflower into florets and lay them in the dish. Mix the béchamel sauce with 1/2 a cup of the Parmesan and the nutmeg. Pour over the cauliflower and sprinkle liberally with the remaining Parmesan. Bake for 20 minutes. At the end of the cooking time, turn on the broiler. Broil the cauliflower until the top turns golden brown.

VARIATION:
Broccoli may be used instead of cauliflower, or the two may be mixed together in the baking dish. This is both eye-catching and tasty.

Melanzane alla Contadina
EGGPLANT BOATS

8 servings – preparation 15 min. – cooking time 40 min.

This is an extremely quick, easy, and versatile dish. It can be either a main meal accompanied with a crusty loaf of bread, or a vegetable dish to go alongside any roast. The flavors of its simple ingredients are perfectly balanced, making it truly scrumptious.

---

4 SMALL EGGPLANTS
DRIED OREGANO
SALT
TOMATOES, AS PREPARED IN TOMATO AND HERB CROSTINI
   (PAGE 14)
4 OUNCES MOZZARELLA, DICED (OPTIONAL)
3 TABLESPOONS GRATED PARMESAN CHEESE (OPTIONAL)

Preheat the oven to 400°F. Rinse and dry the eggplants. Remove and discard the stems, and cut in half lengthwise. Deeply score the exposed flesh of each half with a sharp knife. Sprinkle with salt and oregano. Place the eggplants, scored side up, in a baking pan. Spoon the tomato mixture over them, making sure the mixture fills the scores. Bake for 40 minutes or until soft.

VARIATION:
At the end of the cooking time, sprinkle some diced mozzarella and freshly grated Parmesan over the boats. Place under a hot broiler for 3 minutes before serving, until the cheese has melted.

Melanzane alla griglia

EGGPLANT WITH HERBS AND OLIVE OIL

8 servings – preparation 15 min. – cooking time 10 min.

This is a great summer meal and is very tasty accompanied by fresh cold cuts, cheese, and a crusty loaf of bread.

---

3 LARGE EGGPLANTS, STALKS REMOVED, CUT LENGTHWISE INTO
   $1/3$-INCH-THICK SLICES
2 CUPS OLIVE OIL
2 CLOVES GARLIC, FINELY CHOPPED
3 TABLESPOONS CHOPPED FRESH PARSLEY
SALT
RED WINE VINEGAR TO TASTE

Preheat the broiler. Lay the eggplant slices on a large baking sheet. Place on the highest rack, under the broiler. Broil for 5 minutes on each side, or until they have a mottled effect (but are not burnt). Transfer them to a cooling rack. Drizzle some oil in the bottom of a rectangular airtight container and make layers, starting with the eggplant slices, then the garlic and parsley, salt, vinegar, and more oil. Completely cover the eggplant with the remaining olive oil. In this way it will keep for a month and be on standby for a quick side dish. The eggplant must be completely submerged under the olive oil or it will not keep. It is not necessary to keep this dish in the refrigerator.

VARIATION:
Zucchini can also be prepared this way and are equally divine.

Involtini di Melanzane

EGGPLANT ROLLS

6 servings – preparation 20 min. – cooking time 15 min.

These make a wonderful side dish or light lunch.

---

2 LARGE EGGPLANTS, STALKS REMOVED, CUT LENGTHWISE INTO
   12 THIN SLICES
6 THIN SLICES COOKED HAM, HALVED LENGTHWISE
2 (8-OUNCE) PACKAGES MOZZARELLA, DICED
SALT AND BLACK PEPPER
2 EGGS, BEATEN
1 CUP DRY BREAD CRUMBS
2 CUPS VEGETABLE OIL
TOOTHPICKS

On each slice of eggplant, put half a slice of ham, some diced mozzarella, and a sprinkling of salt and freshly ground pepper. Tightly roll up the slices lengthwise and secure each with two toothpicks. Dip in the beaten egg and then in the bread crumbs. Heat the vegetable oil in a large non-stick skillet and fry the rolls, until golden on all sides. Place on paper toweling to absorb any excess oil, and serve immediately.

Finocchi alla Parmigiana
BAKED FENNEL WITH PARMESAN

6 servings – preparation 15 min. – cooking time 40 min.

This versatile side dish can accompany any meal. The subtle flavor of fennel brings to mind aniseed and contrasts deliciously with the Parmesan.

---

5 FENNEL BULBS
1 TABLESPOON SALT (OR TO TASTE)
¼ CUP BUTTER
½ CUP FRESHLY GRATED PARMESAN CHEESE

Preheat the oven to 400°F. Cut the top off each fennel bulb and slice off a quarter of an inch at the stem. Discard the outer layer and wash thoroughly. Cut lengthwise into quarters. Boil the fennel quarters in salted water for 20 minutes. They should be tender when pierced with a fork. Drain the fennel and lay in a 12 x 9-inch baking pan. Dot with butter and sprinkle liberally with the freshly grated Parmesan. Bake for 20 minutes, or until the top is golden.

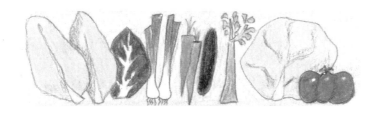

Finocchi al Forno di Carla

CARLA'S ROAST FENNEL

6 servings – preparation 10 min. – cooking time 1 hr.

This is an appetizing side dish to serve with roast beef or chicken.

---

5 FENNEL BULBS
¼ CUP OLIVE OIL
SALT AND BLACK PEPPER

Preheat the oven to 400°F. Cut the top off each fennel bulb and slice off a quarter of an inch at the stem. Discard the outer layer and wash thoroughly. Thinly slice the fennel lengthwise. In a large mixing bowl, toss the fennel with the olive oil, and salt and pepper to taste. Mix well. Lay evenly in a 12 x 9-inch baking pan and roast for 1 hour, stirring occasionally. At the end of the cooking time, the fennel should be tender when pierced with a fork.

Fagiolini Rifatti

DRESSED GREEN BEANS

6 servings – preparation 15 min. – cooking time 40 min.

Fresh beans have a wonderfully delicate flavor which, in this dish, is enhanced by the tomato and garlic.

2 TABLESPOONS OLIVE OIL
3 CLOVES GARLIC, CHOPPED
1 POUND FRESH GREEN BEANS, TIPS AND STRINGS REMOVED
1 (8-OUNCE) CAN PLUM TOMATOES
1 CUBE VEGETABLE-FLAVOR STOCK
SALT AND BLACK PEPPER

Heat the olive oil in a large nonstick skillet, and gently sauté the garlic until golden. Stir in the beans and tomatoes. Add ¾ cup of water and the stock cube (if you use a stock cube that is very salty, half may be sufficient). Simmer, uncovered, for 40 minutes or until the beans are tender, stirring occasionally. If the water evaporates during the cooking time, add another ½ cup. At the end of the cooking time, the beans will be coated in a light tomato sauce. Adjust the flavor with a little salt and pepper if necessary.

Funghi Fritti

DEEP-FRIED MUSHROOMS

6 servings – preparation 10 min. – cooking time 10 min.

4 CUPS VEGETABLE OIL FOR DEEP-FRYING
1 POUND MEDIUM MUSHROOMS, CLEANED AND CUT INTO LARGE,
   EQUAL-SIZE PIECES
1 CUP FLOUR
SALT

Heat the vegetable oil in a deep, heavy-bottomed pan. Lightly dredge the mushrooms with flour. Test the oil by putting one piece of mushroom in (it should sizzle). When the oil is hot enough, deep-fry the mushrooms for 3 minutes, until golden. Drain on paper toweling and sprinkle with salt. Serve immediately.

Cipolle Saporite
SWEET AND SOUR ONIONS

6 servings – preparation 10 min. – cooking time 1 hr.

¼ CUP OLIVE OIL OR BUTTER
1 POUND SMALL WHITE ONIONS, SKINS REMOVED
3 TEASPOONS BROWN OR GRANULATED SUGAR
1 TEASPOON SALT
1 TEASPOON BLACK PEPPER
¼ CUP RED WINE VINEGAR

Heat the olive oil or butter in a large nonstick skillet, and add the onions and 1¾ cups of water. Cook over low heat for 30 minutes, stirring occasionally. Add the remaining ingredients and stir well. Cook, uncovered, for another 30 minutes, stirring occasionally. If the water has reduced, add another ⅓ cup of water. When the sauce has reduced to a syrupy consistency, and the onions are caramel color, place in a warm serving dish. Serve with your choice of roasted meat and potatoes.

Piselli con Prosciutto

PEAS AND HAM

6 servings – preparation 15 min. – cooking time 30 min.

3 TABLESPOONS OLIVE OIL
½ ONION, CHOPPED
1½ CUPS DICED COOKED HAM
1 POUND SMALL PEAS, FRESH OR FROZEN, THAWED AND DRAINED
2 PLUM TOMATOES, CHOPPED
1 TABLESPOON CHOPPED FRESH PARSLEY
1 TABLESPOON CHOPPED FRESH BASIL
½ CUBE VEGETABLE-FLAVOR STOCK
SALT AND BLACK PEPPER

Heat the olive oil in a medium-size nonstick saucepan and lightly sauté the onion and ham for 3 minutes. Add the peas, tomatoes, herbs, and the ½ cube of stock. Mix together, then add ¾ cup of water. Cover the pan and simmer for 30 minutes, until the peas are tender. Salt to taste; not much (if any) will be needed as both the ham and the stock contain salt. Add pepper, if desired.

VARIATIONS:
This dish is not only truly delicious as a vegetable side dish but can also be used as a unique sauce for pasta—refer to Pea and Ham Sauce (page 55).

Vegetarians can leave out the ham, as the peas are also tasty without.

Broad beans can be used as an excellent substitute for the peas.

Peperonata
SAVORY PEPPERS

4 servings – preparation 10 min. – cooking time 20 min.

¼ CUP OLIVE OIL
4 LARGE BELL PEPPERS (RED, YELLOW, AND GREEN), SEEDED AND
   THINLY SLICED
3 CLOVES GARLIC, COARSELY CHOPPED
SALT AND BLACK PEPPER
¼ CUP CAPERS
½ CUP GREEN OLIVES

In a nonstick pan, heat the olive oil and add the peppers and garlic.
Cook for 10 to 15 minutes over medium heat without covering the pan
or adding water. As they cook, gently turn with a wooden spoon, making
sure they don't stick. Don't overcook, as the peppers tend to disintegrate
and become mushy. Before turning off the heat, add salt and pepper to
taste. Add the capers and olives and mix well. This dish may be served
hot or cold.

VARIATION:
These peppers are very tasty served on toasted bread rounds.

Polpette di Patate

ITALIAN POTATO CAKES

6 servings – preparation 1 hr. – cooking time 10 min.

Aside from being a very useful way of using up leftovers, potato cakes are perfect for children who are difficult eaters and constitute a very wholesome meal. The meat is finely ground, making the cakes easy to chew and swallow. Although they take some time to prepare, they cook quickly and are well worth the effort.

---

3 CUPS COOKED BEEF, CHICKEN OR PORK, FINELY GROUND

3 CUPS MASHED POTATOES

2 LARGE CARROTS OR ANY OTHER FAVORITE VEGETABLE, COOKED
   AND MASHED

8 OUNCES FONTINA CHEESE, GRATED

2 EGGS, BEATEN

SALT

2 CUPS DRY BREAD CRUMBS

2 CUPS VEGETABLE OIL FOR FRYING

Combine the meat, potatoes, carrots, cheese, eggs and salt to taste. If the mixture is too soft, keep adding bread crumbs until it is firm enough to make into potato cakes. Place some of the mixture onto the palm of your hand, make a ball (the size of a small lemon), and then flatten it slightly. Coat the potato cake in bread crumbs. Repeat the process with the remaining mixture. Heat the vegetable oil in a nonstick skillet over medium heat. Fry the potato cakes for 5 minutes on each side, or until golden brown. Serve with a salad.

VARIATION:

Potato cakes are equally as good baked in the oven. Preheat the oven to 400°F. Place them on a flat baking sheet and bake for 30 minutes.

Patate con Mozzarella

POTATOES WITH MOZZARELLA

6 servings – preparation 25 min. – cooking time 40 min.

5 LARGE BOILING POTATOES, THINLY SLICED
1 (8-OUNCE) PACKAGE MOZZARELLA, DICED
1½ CUPS DICED COOKED HAM
1 CUP GRATED PARMESAN CHEESE
2 PLUM TOMATOES, DICED
3 TABLESPOONS OLIVE OIL
SALT
¼ CUP CHOPPED FRESH PARSLEY

Preheat the oven to 350°F. Lightly grease the bottom of a 9 x 12-inch roasting pan. Place a third of the potatoes and a ½ cup of water in the bottom and cover them with a third of the mozzarella, ham, Parmesan, tomatoes, and a sprinkling of salt and parsley. Repeat the process, making three layers. Drizzle the top of the casserole with the olive oil. Bake, uncovered, for 40 minutes, or until the top is golden.

Patate Arrosto

ROASTED POTATOES

6 servings – preparation 10 min. – cooking time 1 hr.

English-style roasted potatoes are cut into bigger pieces and usually roasted in sunflower oil. These potatoes are enhanced by the olive oil, salt, and rosemary. The aroma produced while they are roasting is truly mouthwatering.

6 LARGE ROASTING POTATOES, PEELED AND CUT INTO
  BITE-SIZE PIECES
2 TABLESPOONS OLIVE OIL
2 TEASPOONS SALT
1 TEASPOON FRESHLY GROUND BLACK PEPPER
1 SPRIG FRESH ROSEMARY
3 LEAVES FRESH SAGE, ROUGHLY CHOPPED
4 CLOVES GARLIC, PEELED

Preheat the oven to 425°F. In a roasting pan, mix the potatoes with the olive oil and sprinkle them liberally with the salt and black pepper. Add the rosemary, sage and garlic. Place in the oven and roast for 1 hour, making sure to turn them occasionally.

VARIATIONS:
Add slightly larger pieces of pumpkin or winter squash to roast alongside the potatoes (larger, because the pumpkin or squash is softer and cooks quicker). Other options include sliced carrots, cauliflower florets (cauliflower cooks in less time; check it after 30 minutes, it should be lightly browned and tender), and whole onions (cut a deep cross in the top of each). Stir occasionally and test with a fork for tenderness. These are all delectable served alongside any roasted meat.

Spinaci Saltati in Padella
SPINACH WITH GARLIC AND OIL

4 servings – preparation 10 min. – cooking time 5 min.

This is a quick and easy vegetable dish that can accompany roasted meats.

¼ CUP OLIVE OIL
1 CLOVE GARLIC, CUT INTO 3 OR 4 PIECES
2 CUPS COOKED SPINACH
SALT AND BLACK PEPPER
1 TEASPOON GROUND NUTMEG (OPTIONAL)

Heat the olive oil in a large nonstick saucepan, and gently sauté the garlic. Add the spinach and stir gently. Add salt, pepper and, if you like, some freshly ground nutmeg.

VARIATIONS:
You may wish to jazz this dish up by adding crumbled bacon, along with the garlic.

Our children love it when we add cubed Swiss cheese or grated Parmesan at the end of the cooking time. Stir in the cheese until melted.

Pomodori Ripieni con Riso
STUFFED TOMATOES WITH RICE

6 servings – preparation 40 min. – cooking time 1 hr.

This is one of the tastiest of Tuscan recipes we know and a family favorite. Diane's mother-in-law, Maria Nocentini, prefers to cook this dish in the summer, when the tomatoes are fresh from the garden. It is a little time consuming to prepare but well worth the effort. We suggest making a double recipe, as the tomatoes will keep in the fridge for up to 4 days and are a quick meal for another day. They can be served hot or cold.

---

12 TABLESPOONS UNCOOKED WHITE RICE (ONE FOR EACH
    STUFFED TOMATO)
14 MEDIUM TOMATOES
$\frac{1}{2}$ CUP CHOPPED FRESH BASIL
2 TABLESPOONS CHOPPED FRESH PARSLEY
$\frac{1}{4}$ CUP DRIED OREGANO
3 CLOVES GARLIC, CHOPPED
1 CUP OLIVE OIL
SALT AND BLACK PEPPER
$\frac{3}{4}$ CUP WHITE WINE

Preheat the oven to 400°F. In a small saucepan, boil 4 cups of water. Add the rice and boil for 5 minutes only. Drain immediately. Cut off the tops of 12 tomatoes and reserve. Carefully spoon out all the pulp. In a blender, blend the pulp with the remaining 2 tomatoes. Add the herbs and chopped garlic, and blend. To this mixture add 5 tablespoons of olive oil and a good sprinkling of salt and pepper. Add the rice to the tomato mixture and mix well. Fill the hollowed tomatoes with the mixture. If any is left over, just spoon it into the bottom of a 9 x 12-inch baking pan, along with the white wine. Don't worry if the mixture looks a little watery inside the tomatoes, as during the cooking time all the liquid will be absorbed by the rice. Put the tops back on the tomatoes, and place them in a single layer in the baking pan. Add another 5 tablespoons of olive oil to the bottom of the pan, and sprinkle the lidded tomatoes liberally with salt. Bake for 1 hour on the lowest rack of the oven. During the cooking time, baste the tomatoes with the juices from the bottom of the pan.

VARIATION:
We often put diced potatoes around the tomatoes. They cook in the juice and are quite delectable.

Pomodori Ripieni con Parmigiano
STUFFED TOMATOES WITH PARMESAN

6 servings – preparation 20 min. – cooking time 20 min.

Tomatoes are also delicious stuffed with a mix of Parmesan, bread crumbs and herbs. This is a great side dish to serve at your next barbecue.

---

12 MEDIUM TOMATOES
1 CUP GRATED PECORINO OR PARMESAN CHEESE
1 CUP DRY BREAD CRUMBS
1 TABLESPOON OF SALT
$\frac{1}{2}$ CUP CHOPPED BASIL
$\frac{1}{4}$ CUP DRIED OREGANO
6 BLACK PITTED OLIVES, SLICED IN HALF

Preheat oven to 400°F. Slice the tomatoes in half and spoon out the inside of each half. Combine the tomato pulp with the cheese, bread crumbs, salt, basil and oregano. Fill each tomato half and decorate each top with $\frac{1}{2}$ an olive. Bake for 45 minutes.

VARIATION:
If you are short on time another alternative is to cut the tomatoes in half and sprinkle with a little salt, dry bread crumbs, grated Parmesan, and dried oregano. Broil until the top turns golden, and serve.

Zucchini Fritti

DEEP-FRIED ZUCCHINI

6 servings – preparation 15 min. – cooking time 15 min.

---

4 CUPS VEGETABLE OIL FOR DEEP-FRYING
1 EGG, BEATEN
SALT AND BLACK PEPPER
4 MEDIUM ZUCCHINI, SLICED INTO $\frac{1}{4}$-INCH DISCS OR
   LENGTHWISE INTO $\frac{1}{4}$-INCH THICK STICKS
$\frac{1}{2}$ CUP DRY BREAD CRUMBS

Heat the vegetable oil in a deep, heavy-bottomed pan. Combine the egg with salt and pepper to taste. Dip the zucchini pieces into the egg mixture and coat them with the bread crumbs. Test the oil by putting one piece of zucchini in—it should sizzle. When the oil is hot enough, deep-fry the zucchini pieces for 7 minutes, or until golden. Drain on paper toweling and sprinkle with salt. Serve immediately.

Zucchine in Umido
TOMATO AND BASIL ZUCCHINI

6 servings – preparation 15 min. – cooking time 20 min.

2 TABLESPOONS OLIVE OIL
1 ONION, CHOPPED
5 MEDIUM ZUCCHINI, DICED
1 TABLESPOON CHOPPED FRESH BASIL
2 FRESH OR CANNED PLUM TOMATOES, CHOPPED
$\frac{1}{2}$ CUBE VEGETABLE FLAVOR STOCK
SALT AND BLACK PEPPER TO TASTE

Heat the olive oil in a nonstick pan, and sauté the onion. When it is translucent, add the zucchini. Mix well and cook for 5 minutes. Add the remaining ingredients and $\frac{1}{3}$ cup of water. Cover the pan and simmer for 20 minutes.

VARIATIONS:
This dish is extremely versatile, as it can also be used as a sauce for pasta and as a base for poached eggs. Refer to Tomato and Basil Zucchini Sauce (page 55) and Poached Eggs with Tomato and Basil Zucchini (page 125).

Zucchini Ripieni

STUFFED ZUCCHINI

6 servings – preparation 40 min. – cooking time 1 hr.

6 LARGE ZUCCHINI, HALVED LENGTHWISE
1 CUP DICED HAM
1 CLOVE GARLIC, CHOPPED
1 EGG, BEATEN
½ CUP GRATED PARMESAN CHEESE
½ CUP DRY BREAD CRUMBS
3 TABLESPOONS CHOPPED FRESH PARSLEY
⅓ CUP OLIVE OIL
SALT AND BLACK PEPPER
¼ CUP TOMATO SAUCE

Preheat the oven to 350°F. With an apple corer remove the pulp from the halved zucchini, leaving little boats. Chop the pulp. In a large mixing bowl, combine the pulp, ham, garlic, egg, ¼ cup of Parmesan, ¼ cup of bread crumbs, parsley, olive oil and a liberal amount of salt and pepper. To the bottom of a greased 9 x 12-inch baking pan, add the tomato sauce and ⅓ cup of water. Fill the boats with the pulp mixture and place them side by side in the pan. Sprinkle generously with the remaining Parmesan and bread crumbs before placing in the oven for 1 hour or until crispy and golden on top.

TIP:
These ingredients can be mixed in a blender but we have found the texture is better when they are finely chopped.

6 LARGE ZUCCHINI
2 TABLESPOONS OLIVE OIL
2 SMALL ONIONS, CHOPPED
3 SLICES COOKED HAM, CHOPPED
1 EGG, BEATEN
½ CUP DRY BREAD CRUMBS
1 CUP GRATED PECORINO CHEESE
SALT
1 TEASPOON DRIED OREGANO

Preheat oven to 350°F. In a large saucepan of boiling water, boil 6 whole zucchini for 5 minutes, drain, and allow to cool. In a skillet, heat 2 tablespoons of olive oil and gently sauté the onions and ham. Cut each zucchini in half lengthwise. With an apple corer, remove the pulp, leaving little boats. Combine the pulp of the zucchini with the onions, ham, egg, ¼ cup dry bread crumbs, ½ cup of Pecorino cheese, salt to taste, and oregano. Fill the zucchini boats with the pulp mixture and place in a baking dish. Sprinkle the remaining Pecorino and bread crumbs over the top, and bake for 45 minutes or until golden.

Dolci

DESSERTS AND SWEET CRÊPES

We have taken a few liberties in our dessert chapter. Many of the recipes are not typically Tuscan, but they are what we have enjoyed making and eating since having moved to Italy. The following is a selection of recipes which our Tuscan friends and family have shared with us. We have included only the most irresistible, and only those we make on a regular basis.

Torta di Mele
APPLE CAKE

1 10-inch cake – preparation 30 min. – baking time 40 min.

This cake is delicately light and spongy, and adds a touch of class to any occasion.

2¼ CUPS ALL-PURPOSE FLOUR
1 CUP GRANULATED SUGAR
1 TABLESPOON BAKING POWDER
4 EGGS, BEATEN
1 CUP BUTTER, MELTED
¾ CUP WHOLE MILK
2 APPLES, PEELED AND THINLY SLICED
CONFECTIONERS' SUGAR

Preheat the oven to 350°F. Grease and flour a 10-inch-diameter springform or nonstick cake pan. Sift the flour, granulated sugar, and baking powder into a mixing bowl. In a separate bowl, mix the beaten eggs, melted butter, and milk. Pour into the dry ingredients and mix well. Pour the batter into the prepared cake pan. Arrange the apple slices decoratively on the top of the cake. Place the pan on the lowest rack of the oven, and do not open the oven door during the baking time, or the center of the cake will sink. Bake for 40 minutes, or until an inserted toothpick comes out dry. Leave the cake to cool and then take it out of the pan. Place the cake on a serving plate, and sprinkle with confectioners' sugar.

Torta di Banana

BANANA CAKE

1 10-inch cake – preparation 25 min. – baking time 45 min.

This is a great cake accompanied by hot milky coffee in the morning or served with afternoon tea.

---

3 CUPS ALL-PURPOSE FLOUR
½ TEASPOON SALT
4 TEASPOONS BAKING POWDER
2 EGGS
1 CUP GRANULATED SUGAR
½ CUP BUTTER, MELTED
GRATED ZEST OF 1 LEMON
GRATED ZEST OF 1 ORANGE
1 BANANA, MASHED
1 APPLE, GRATED
1 TABLESPOON ROUGHLY CHOPPED BLANCHED ALMONDS
CONFECTIONERS' SUGAR

Preheat the oven to 350°F. Grease and flour a 10-inch-diameter spring-form or nonstick cake pan. Sift the flour, salt, and baking powder into a large mixing bowl. In a separate bowl, beat the eggs and mix with the sugar, melted butter, lemon and orange rinds, banana, and apple, then transfer to the bowl with the dry ingredients. Mix well and pour the batter into the prepared pan. Sprinkle with the almonds, and bake for 45 minutes, or until an inserted toothpick comes out dry. Leave the cake to cool and then take it out of the pan. Place the cake on a serving plate, and sprinkle with confectioners' sugar.

VARIATIONS:
If you prefer a straightforward banana flavor, omit the lemon and orange zest and the apple; add an extra mashed banana instead.

If you are a chocolate lover, add a cup of chocolate morsels. Children love banana chip cake.

Torta di Formaggio

ITALIAN CHEESECAKE

1 8-inch cake – preparation 20 min. – baking time 1 hr.

This is a classic cheesecake that is delightfully light. Be adventurous and try different toppings. Orange, strawberry, or forest fruit sauce are three tasty options.

2 CUPS CRUSHED GRAHAM CRACKERS
½ CUP (1 STICK) BUTTER, MELTED
1 TEASPOON GROUND CINNAMON
1¼ CUPS RICOTTA CHEESE
1¼ CUPS CREAM CHEESE
1¼ CUPS MASCARPONE CHEESE
GRATED ZEST OF 1 ORANGE
2 EGGS
1 CUP SUGAR
2 TABLESPOONS CREAMY CHOCOLATE HAZELNUT SPREAD
   (NUTELLA)
2 TABLESPOONS MILK

Combine the crushed crackers, melted butter, and cinnamon. Form a crust on the bottom of an 8-inch-diameter springform cake pan with this mixture. Chill in the fridge for 30 minutes. Preheat the oven to 350°F. Beat together the cheeses, orange zest, eggs, and sugar until smooth. Pour over the chilled graham cracker base and bake for 1 hour. Let the cheesecake cool and then chill it in the fridge for 2 hours. Combine the chocolate hazelnut spread and milk, creating a creamy topping, and spread it evenly over the top of the cheesecake. Serve.

Torta di Cioccolata

CLASSIC CHOCOLATE CAKE

1 10-inch cake – preparation 20 min. – baking time 45 min.

This cake is deliciously moist and requires no icing.

4-OUNCES DARK CHOCOLATE, SEMISWEET
$\frac{1}{2}$ CUP BOILING WATER
1 CUP BUTTER, ROOM TEMPERATURE
2 CUPS SUGAR
4 EGGS, SEPARATED
$\frac{1}{2}$ CUP WHOLE MILK
$2\frac{1}{2}$ CUPS ALL-PURPOSE FLOUR
2 TEASPOONS BAKING POWDER
1 TEASPOON SALT

Preheat oven to 350°F. Grease and flour an 11-inch-diameter springform or nonstick cake pan. Break the chocolate into a small mixing bowl and pour the boiling water over it. Stir until melted and set aside to cool. In a separate bowl, cream the butter and sugar, and add the egg yolks. Mix well. Add the chocolate and stir until smooth. Add the milk and mix well. Into a third bowl, sift the flour, baking powder, and salt. Combine the wet and dry ingredients, and mix until smooth. Beat the egg whites until soft peaks form. Fold gently into the batter. Pour the batter into the prepared pan. Bake for 45 minutes, or until an inserted toothpick comes out dry. Leave the cake to cool and then take it out of the pan. Place the cake on a serving plate. A light sprinkling of confectioners' sugar adds a nice finishing touch.

VARIATIONS:
Though this cake needs no icing, if you wish to indulge in a few extra calories, a creamy chocolate or coconut butter pecan icing will do nicely.

This cake is also suitable for serving as Black Forest chocolate cake. Cut the cake in half horizontally. Spread canned cherry pie filling between the layers. Top with fresh whipped cream, and garnish with chocolate shavings.

Torta di Cocco

COCONUT CAKE

1 10-inch cake – preparation 20 min. – baking time 40 min.

1¾ CUPS ALL-PURPOSE FLOUR
1¼ CUPS GRANULATED SUGAR
1 TEASPOON BAKING POWDER
4 EGGS, BEATEN
2¾ CUPS DRY COCONUT, UNSWEETENED
1 CUP WHOLE MILK
⅔ CUP BUTTER, MELTED
CONFECTIONERS' SUGAR

Preheat the oven to 350°F. Grease and flour a 10-inch-diameter spring-form or nonstick cake pan. Sift the flour, sugar, and baking powder in a large mixing bowl. Add all the remaining ingredients, except for the confectioners' sugar. Mix well and pour the batter into the prepared pan. Bake for 40 minutes, or until an inserted toothpick comes out dry. Leave the cake to cool and then take it out of the pan. Place the cake on a serving plate, and sprinkle with confectioners' sugar.

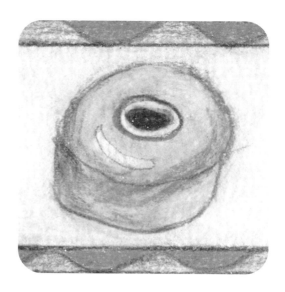

Torta di Ananas

PINEAPPLE CAKE

1 10-inch cake – preparation 25 min. – baking time 35 min.

1 (8-OUNCE) CAN PINEAPPLE RINGS, DRAINED WELL
1½ CUPS ALL-PURPOSE FLOUR
1¼ CUPS GRANULATED SUGAR
4 TEASPOONS BAKING POWDER
4 EGGS, BEATEN
½ CUP BUTTER, MELTED
CONFECTIONERS' SUGAR

Preheat the oven to 350°F. Line a 10-inch-diameter springform cake pan with waxed paper. Arrange the pineapple rings in the lined pan, making sure there is no juice. Sift the flour, sugar, and baking powder into a mixing bowl. Add the beaten eggs and the melted butter. Mix well. Spread this mixture evenly over the pineapple rings. Place the pan on the lowest rack of the oven and bake for 35 minutes, or until an inserted toothpick comes out dry. Do not open the oven door during the baking time, or the cake will sink. Once baked, turn the cake over onto a heat-proof serving plate, removing the pan and the waxed paper. Under a hot broiler, lightly brown the top of the cake, being careful not to burn it. When cooled, sprinkle with confectioners' sugar.

Biscotti al Cocco

COCONUT COOKIES

2¹/₂ dozen – preparation 20 min. – chilling time 1 hr.

2½ CUPS CRUSHED GRAHAM CRACKERS
1¾ CUPS SUGAR
3 EGGS, BEATEN (THE FINISHED RECIPE CONTAINS RAW EGGS)
1 CUP BUTTER, MELTED
3½ CUPS DRY COCONUT, UNSWEETENED
2 TABLESPOONS RUM
⅓ CUP UNSWEETENED COCOA POWDER

Combine all the ingredients in a mixing bowl. Take heaping tablespoons of the mixture in the palm of your hand, and form into 30 balls. Place the cookies on a baking sheet and place in the fridge. Chill for 1 hour and serve.

Biscotti ai Cornflakes

CORNFLAKE COOKIES

2½ dozen – preparation 30 min. – baking time 10 min.

3 EGGS
1¼ CUPS GRANULATED SUGAR
¾ CUP BUTTER, MELTED
¾ CUP PINE NUTS
1 TEASPOON VANILLA EXTRACT
A PINCH OF SALT
2¼ CUPS ALL-PURPOSE FLOUR
2 TEASPOONS BAKING POWDER
3 CUPS OF CORNFLAKES
CONFECTIONERS' SUGAR

Preheat the oven to 350°F. Grease baking sheets. In a mixing bowl, beat the eggs and mix in the granulated sugar, melted butter, pine nuts, vanilla extract, salt, flour, and baking powder. Use a tablespoon of batter for each cookie. Form into balls, and roll in the cornflakes, until completely covered. Place them on the prepared baking sheets, and bake for 10 minutes, until golden. Sprinkle cooled cookies with confectioners' sugar.

Macedonia di Frutta

FRUIT SALAD

6 servings – preparation 25 min.

JUICE OF 4 LEMONS
1 BANANA
1 LARGE APPLE
1 LARGE PEAR
¼ POUND STRAWBERRIES
2 PEACHES
2 APRICOTS
1 SLICE HONEYDEW MELON
2 KIWIS
5 TABLESPOONS SUGAR, OR TO TASTE

Pour the lemon juice into a large glass serving bowl. Peel and slice or dice the fruit into bite-size pieces, and mix in with the lemon juice. Add the sugar and ⅓ cup of water. These amounts may vary, depending on the sweetness of the fruits and the amount of their juices. Chill slightly and serve.

VARIATION:
We also enjoy adding a little fruit liqueur, Grand Marnier for example, to enhance the scintillating flavors.

Semifreddo al Caffè
COFFEE PARFAIT

8 servings – preparation 15 min. – freezing time 6 hr.

This dessert is so irresistible, we've even had friends on diets asking for a second helping!

---

3 EGGS, SEPARATED (THE FINISHED RECIPE CONTAINS RAW EGGS)
2 CUPS WHIPPING CREAM
1 (1-POUND) PACKAGE LADYFINGERS
1¼ CUPS PREPARED ESPRESSO, COOLED
1¼ CUPS SUGAR
CHOCOLATE-COVERED COFFEE BEANS (GARNISH)
CHOCOLATE SHAVINGS (GARNISH)

Beat the egg whites until soft peaks form. In a separate bowl, beat the cream until soft peaks form. Soak the ladyfingers in 1 cup of the espresso and use them to line a deep dessert dish, placing one layer horizontally on the bottom, and vertically up the sides. In a deep mixing bowl, beat the egg yolks, sugar, and the remaining ¼ cup of espresso. Once smooth, gently fold in the egg whites and the cream, until completely blended and creamy. Pour this mixture into the ladyfinger-lined dish, cover with plastic wrap, and freeze for 6 hours. Remove from your freezer 15 minutes before serving. Once you have turned out the dessert onto an attractive serving plate, decorate with chocolate-covered coffee beans and chocolate shavings.

TIP:
This dessert can be made the day before serving.

Pesche alla Crema

PEACHES AND CREAM

4 servings – preparation 30 min. – cooking time 10 min.

---

4 PEACHES, PEELED, HALVED, AND PITTED
⅓ CUP PLUS 1 TABLESPOON SUGAR
½ CUP WHITE WINE
1 CUP WHIPPING CREAM
1 EGG
1 TABLESPOON ALL-PURPOSE FLOUR
1 CUP WHOLE MILK

Place the peaches in a nonstick saucepan with ⅓ cup of the sugar and the white wine. Simmer for 10 minutes. Take the peaches out of the saucepan and reserve the liquid. Divide the peaches into four dessert dishes. Whip the cream until firm peaks form. Mix together the egg, remaining 1 tablespoon of sugar, flour, and milk. In a nonstick saucepan, bring this mixture to a boil, stirring continuously for 5 minutes. Once the custard has cooled, gently fold in the whipped cream and divide it evenly over the peaches in the four dishes. Drizzle over each a little of the juice that the peaches have cooked in. Chill for 30 minutes and serve.

Pasta Bignè
CHOUX PASTRY

4 dozen – preparation 30 min. – cooking time 15 min.

⅓ CUP BUTTER
A PINCH OF SALT
1⅓ CUPS ALL-PURPOSE FLOUR
5 EGGS

Preheat the oven to 350°F. Bring to a boil 1½ cups of water in a nonstick saucepan with the butter and a pinch of salt. Turn off the heat, and gradually stir in the flour, mixing continuously, until the mixture is firm and smooth. Add one egg at a time, stirring each one into the mixture until smooth. A lot of "elbow grease" will be needed when mixing. It may seem that the egg will never be completely blended in, you just have to keep going and trust that it will be. The mixture is ready when it comes away from the sides of the bowl, and is a soft creamy consistency. Spoon the mixture into a piping bag, and pipe little balls (each about the size of a large walnut) onto a greased baking sheet. Space the balls one inch apart. Bake in the oven for fifteen minutes, or until golden. Once they are cool take them off the baking sheet and fill them as you wish. (See recipes pages 166 and 167.)

Bongo

CHOCOLATE-COVERED PROFITEROLES

8 servings – preparation 30 min.

1 CUP WHIPPING CREAM
2 TABLESPOONS CONFECTIONERS' SUGAR
2 DOZEN SMALL ROUND PROFITEROLES (CHOUX PASTRY,
   PAGE 165)
2 CUPS CREAMY CHOCOLATE HAZELNUT SPREAD (NUTELLA)
¾ CUP WHOLE MILK

Whip the cream and add the confectioners' sugar until stiff peaks form. Spoon the whipped cream into a piping bag fitted with a large nozzle. Make a small hole in each profiterole with the end of the nozzle and fill them with the sweetened cream. Place in a pyramid on a serving plate. Put the chocolate hazelnut spread into a mixing bowl and gradually add the milk, stirring continuously until it has a creamy consistency. Pour the mixture over and into the gaps of the pyramid, so that it is well covered, and serve.

Bongo alla Crema
CUSTARD-FILLED PROFITEROLES

8 servings – preparation 40 min.

Profiteroles are also delectable with a custard filling.

¾ CUP SUGAR
6 EGG YOLKS
2 TEASPOONS VANILLA EXTRACT
½ CUP ALL-PURPOSE FLOUR
2⅓ CUPS WHOLE MILK
¼ CUP BUTTER
2 DOZEN SMALL ROUND PROFITEROLES (CHOUX PASTRY,
    PAGE 165)

In a heavy-bottomed pot, cream the sugar, yolks, and vanilla until smooth. Sift the flour and add gradually. Stir into a smooth paste. Over medium heat, gradually add the milk to the paste, stirring continuously, and bring to a boil. Add the butter. Lower the heat, keeping the mixture at a gentle boil. Whisk for 2 minutes, allowing the mixture to thicken. Remove from heat. When the mixture is cool, fill the icing bag (use a large nozzle) and continue as in the previous recipe. If you have any custard left over, use in a piping bag to decorate your pyramid.

VARIATION:
You can also use this cream to fill sweet crêpes. Sprinkle a little cocoa powder and confectioners' sugar over the top before serving.

Crostata

JAM TART

1 10-inch tart – preparation 15 min. – baking time 35 min.

This is a really quick and easy tart. We like it because it doesn't resemble a traditional jam tart, with a layer of pastry and then a layer of jam. This tart is similar to a cake, as the pastry and jam intermingle while cooking.

2½ CUPS ALL-PURPOSE FLOUR
1 CUP SUGAR
4 TEASPOONS BAKING POWDER
3 EGGS, BEATEN
½ CUP OLIVE OIL
GRATED ZEST OF 1 LEMON
6 TABLESPOONS JAM

Preheat the oven to 325°F. Line a 10-inch-diameter springform cake pan with waxed paper. Sift the flour, sugar, and baking powder into a mixing bowl. Add the beaten eggs, olive oil, and lemon zest. Mix well. Spread the mixture on the bottom of the prepared pan. Spoon the jam over the dough, and bake for 35 minutes, or until an inserted toothpick comes out dry.

VARIATION:
Instead of baking in one large pan, you may divide the mixture between two smaller pans, putting a different type of jam on each.

Crostata di Marmellata Tradizionale

TRADITIONAL JAM TART

1 10 ½-inch tart – preparation 30 min. – rest 30 min. – bake 30 min.

3 CUPS ALL-PURPOSE FLOUR
1¼ CUPS SUGAR
1 TEASPOON BAKING POWDER
2 EGGS, BEATEN
¾ CUP BUTTER, SOFTENED
GRATED ZEST OF 1 LEMON
2 CUPS JAM

Sift the flour, sugar and baking powder into a large mixing bowl. Add all the other ingredients except the jam to the bowl, and working with your hands, gently incorporate them. For best results, try not to knead the dough more than necessary. Cover and let the dough rest for a ½ hour. Preheat the oven to 350°F. Flour a pastry board and roll out two-thirds of the dough until it is ⅓-inch thick and will fit a 10½-inch-diameter flan dish. Line the flan dish with the pastry. Fill the pastry base with the jam topping. Roll out the remaining dough and cut into long strips. Crisscross these strips over the jam to create a lattice effect. Bake for 30 minutes, or until the pastry is golden.

VARIATION:
This pastry also makes excellent cookies. Roll out the dough, until it is ⅓-inch thick, and using cookie cutters, cut into your desired shapes. They can be decorated with pine nuts, almonds, raisins, chocolate morsels, or blobs of jam. Bake in a preheated oven (350°F) for 10 to 12 minutes. Kids love them, especially if they participate in the decorating!

COFFEE TIRAMISU

makes 2, each serving 8 – preparation 30 min. – chilling time 2 hr.

We always make two desserts at a time, freezing one for another occasion. You can make a single tiramisu with half of the following amounts, if you prefer.

---

6 EGGS, SEPARATED (THE FINISHED RECIPE CONTAINS RAW EGGS)
6 TABLESPOONS SUGAR
A PINCH OF SALT
1 (1-POUND) PACKAGE LADYFINGERS
2 CUPS PREPARED ESPRESSO OR STRONG COFFEE, MIXED WITH 6
    TEASPOONS SUGAR
1 (1-POUND) CONTAINER MASCARPONE
UNSWEETENED COCOA POWDER

With an electric mixer, beat the egg yolks with the sugar in a large mixing bowl, until the sugar has dissolved and the mixture is creamy. In another large mixing bowl, beat the egg whites with a pinch of salt, until they form firm peaks. Dip the ladyfingers in the cooled sweetened coffee and line two 10 x 13-inch serving dishes. With the electric mixer, blend the mascarpone with the egg yolks. With a large wooden spoon, gently fold the egg whites into the mascarpone mixture. Spoon the mixture into the lined serving dishes. Dust both dishes with cocoa powder and chill for 2 hours before serving.

Crespelle Dolci
BASIC SWEET CRÊPES

6 servings – preparation 5 min. – resting 1 hr. – cooking time 30 min.

All of the following crêpe recipes are based on filling a dozen crêpes. They will serve a party of six, although after a filling meal one per person should suffice.

¾ CUP ALL-PURPOSE FLOUR
1 CUP WHOLE MILK
3 EGGS, BEATEN
1 TABLESPOON SUGAR
BUTTER

Refer to the method in the Basic Crêpes recipe (page 112). After the batter has been blended and rested for an hour, mix well once again and proceed.

Crespelle con Cioccolato e Banana
CHOCOLATE AND BANANA CRÊPES

6 servings – preparation 30 min. – cooking time 10 min.

SINGLE RECIPE BASIC SWEET CRÊPES (ABOVE)
BUTTER
1 (12-OUNCE) JAR CREAMY CHOCOLATE HAZELNUT SPREAD
  (NUTELLA)
5 BANANAS, SLICED
2 CUPS WHIPPING CREAM, WHIPPED

Preheat the oven to 400°F. Butter a baking dish. Roll up the crêpes with a nice helping of chocolate hazelnut spread and some banana slices inside. Place the crêpes in the baking dish and bake for 10 minutes, until heated through. Decorate with whipped cream.

Crespelle all'Arancia

ORANGE CRÊPES

6 servings – preparation 30 min. – cooking time 10 min.

12 ORANGES, 6 PEELED AND SLICED INTO SMALL PIECES AND 6
  SQUEEZED AND STRAINED OF PULP
2 TABLESPOONS BUTTER
6 TABLESPOONS SUGAR
1 TABLESPOON ORANGE LIQUEUR
SINGLE RECIPE BASIC SWEET CRÊPES (PAGE 171)

Place the orange pieces, orange juice, butter, sugar, and liqueur in a non-stick skillet. Stir the mixture over medium heat. After 2 minutes, remove the orange pieces with a slotted spoon and place in a bowl. Over medium heat, reduce the sauce to a syrupy consistency. Place the crêpes on a warm serving platter and fill each with 3 tablespoons of the orange pieces. Fold each crêpe in half and brush a little syrup over each. Then, fold each over again into a triangle. Pour the remaining sauce over the top and serve.

Crespelle alle Fragole e al Kiwi
STRAWBERRY AND KIWI CRÊPES

6 servings – preparation 30 min. – cooking time 10 min.

SINGLE RECIPE BASIC SWEET CRÊPES (PAGE 171)
BUTTER
20 OUNCES RICOTTA OR MASCARPONE CHEESE
½ POUND STRAWBERRIES, CHOPPED
4 KIWIS, PEELED AND CHOPPED
3 TABLESPOONS SUGAR
WHIPPED CREAM OR VANILLA ICE CREAM

Preheat the oven to 400°F. Butter a baking dish. Roll up the crêpes with a little ricotta cheese, strawberries, and kiwi, and a sprinkling of sugar inside. Place them in the prepared dish and bake for 10 minutes, until heated through. Serve with freshly whipped cream or vanilla ice cream.

VARIATIONS:
Any type of fruit can be used in these crêpes, so be creative. Peaches and apricots are a delicious combination, or you may enjoy "fruit salad" crêpes with strawberries, kiwi, banana, and peaches. Fruits of the forest are another alternative: we enjoy mixing raspberries, strawberries, blackberries, and blueberries. These ideas are all eye-catching and original. To add some color, reserve a little fruit to dot the tops of the heated crêpes or add an artistic touch with some sliced fresh fruit beside the crêpes or on the ice cream.

Vini Toscani

TUSCAN WINE

It can most certainly be said that the wines of Tuscany have no equal. This is not surprising, as the history of Tuscan wine goes back 2,500 years to the times of the Etruscans. They have had plenty of time to develop this art, and the results are renowned the world over. Of course, one may have other preferences, but in the end it all comes down to a matter of taste. The structured, intense flavors of Chianti Classico, Chianti, Vino Nobile di Montpulciano, Carmignano, and Brunello di Montalcino are indisputably among the best.

Over twenty years ago, Chianti was of dubious quality. It was a light everyday wine, often created with predominately red grapes and some white, fermented in chestnut barrels, and sold in straw-covered bottles. Today, the quality of Chianti has changed dramatically and it has become the epitome of Italian red wines. The fertile Tuscan hills, rich in sandstone, marl, and limestone, are caressed by the warm Mediterranean sun and this combination, along with a mild climate and principally Sangiovese grapes, produce this deliciously versatile wine. Many fine Tuscan vineyards also produce wines based upon French grapes, such as Cabernet Sauvignon and Merlot, along with other Italian varieties including Canaiolo Nero, Trebbiano Toscano, and Malvasia Bianca Lunga. The beauty of this wine lies in its versatility—from light table wines for an everyday meal, to the intense bouquet of a reserve such as Nipozzano to celebrate a special occasion, Chianti is the perfect choice. If you are searching for "that special bottle," we have been told (by a reliable source) that 1997, 2000, and 2001 were excellent years. We once heard someone describe a particular glass of Chianti as "angels dancing on my tongue" and having spent a number of years consuming this nectar of the gods, we full-heartedly agree.

The boundaries for the production area of Chianti Classico were established in 1932, and have remained unchanged to this day. There are 6,800 hectares of specialized vineyards that produce this wine. All Chianti Classico has to undergo strict laboratory tests every year to guarantee its quality, characteristic bouquet, and flavor. Only then can the Gallo Nero (Black Rooster) emblem be placed on the bottles. The Gallo Nero Consortium offers the ever-more-demanding consumer a guaranteed top-quality wine.

The alcoholic strength of Chianti Classico wine is 12 percent, whereas the alcoholic strength for reserve wines, after a three-year period of aging, is 12.5 percent. Obviously, the length of time a wine is aged depends on both the type and quality. For example, a supple Morellino di Scansano requires one year, whereas a robust and full-bodied Brunello di Montalcino requires five years. Chianti reserves are aged in oak casks (barrique) for two years, within the ancient cellars of many fine Tuscan vineyards. They are marked D.O.C. or D.O.C.G., denominazione di origine controllata e garantita (place of origin controlled and guaranteed) exclusively. This guarantee promises a superior wine rich in balance and depth. The D.O.C. variety covers much of the central zone of Tuscany, although the true historical zone is between Florence and Siena. Years ago there were few vines per hectare covering these zones, but as the wine producers wanted to boost production, they increased the density of the vines to as many as 5,500 to 6,000 per hectare.

The current selection of Tuscan D.O.C.G. wines is as follows: Brunello di Montalcino, Carmignano, Chianti, Chianti Classico, Vernaccia di San Gimignano, and Vino Nobile di Montepulciano.

The Tuscan D.O.C. category includes: Capalbio, Cortona, Colli di Luni, Candia dei Colli Apuani, Colline Lucchesi, Montecarlo Bianco, Bianco della Valdinievole, Colli dell'Etruria Centrale, Vin Santo del Chianti Classico, Vin Santo Del Chianti, Bianco dell'Empolese, Barco Reale di Carmignano, Pomino, Bianco Pisano di San Torpè, Montescudaio, Bolgheri, Val di Cornia, Elba, San Gimignano, Val d'Arbia, Bianco Vergine Valdichiana, Rosso di Montepulciano, Vin Santo di Montepulciano, Rosso di Montalcino, Moscadello di Montalcino, Sant'Antimo, Morellino di Scansano, Orcia, Bianco di Pitigliano, Parrina, Montecucco, Monteregio di Massa Marittima, Ansonica Costa dell'Argentario, and Sovana.

Other Tuscan wines worth mentioning are: Castiglioni, Rèmole, Sassicaia, Tignanello, Sammarco, Tavernelle, Solaia, Albizzia Chardonnay, Pinot Grigio, Rosa di Corte, and Vermentino della Maremma.

Our advice is, once again, to be adventurous and let your tastebuds guide you. We believe finding a disappointing bottle will require a pleasurable and time-consuming search!

If you are not a wine drinker, a good introduction could be new wine, "Il Novello," which consists of newly crushed grapes that haven't been fermented. It has a juicy, syrupy quality, a lesser alcohol content, and is lightly effervescent.

Vin Santo is a famous D.O.C. dessert wine. It is made with semidried grapes that are hung up after the grape harvest until the New Year. They are then pressed, and the must is fermented in oak casks for four years. It is drunk after a meal and usually served with cantuccini di Prato *(very hard almond cookies)*, which Italians enjoy dunking. This dessert wine has a delicate aroma of vanilla and almonds, with a fragrant bouquet of dried fruit.

A favorite pastime for many wine connoisseurs is discussing which wines to serve with which dishes. We would like to keep this topic as straightforward as possible: the following is offered as only a basic guideline to assist you in your wine selection.

D.O.C.G. WINES:

Brunello di Montalcino	Game, rabbit stew, and aged cheese
Carmignano	Roasted pork and roasted pheasant
Chianti	A young Chianti may be served with sliced meats, and pasta dishes with rich sauces. An aged Chianti is well-suited to red meats, such as broiled steak.
Chianti Classico	Red meats, pot roast, and aged cheese
Vernaccia di San Gimignano	First courses based on pasta, vegetables, and baked fish
Vino Nobile di Montepulciano	Red meats, pheasant, and aged cheese

Other Suggested Wine Combinations:

Beef, grilled or roasted	Intense, medium-aged red
Beef Stew	Robust, aged red
Chicken	Dry white or rosé
Fish, grilled or panfried	Dry white or young, light rosé
Lamb	Dry, medium-bodied red
Omelets	Full-bodied rosé
Pasta, fish-based	Dry or slightly sweet white
Pasta, meat-based	Rosé or young red
Pasta, tomato-based	Dry white
Pasta, vegetable-based	Smooth, dry white
Pie, Vegetable	Structured rosé or young, decisive red
Pork	Dry, medium-bodied red

Rabbit	Light, moderately young red
Rice with mushrooms	Young and refreshing red
Soup, Bean	Light, full-flavored rosé
Soup, Fish	Full-bodied rosé or young red
Soup, Pasta	Light, full-flavored rosé
Soup, Vegetable	Light, full-flavored rosé
Veal	Light, young red

In General:

Beef	Base the age and structure of your red wine on the dish you are serving.
Cheese	If fresh and delicate, offer a white wine. If mature and rich, offer a red wine.
Dessert	Offer a sweet dessert wine.
Fruit or raw vegetables	Do not serve any kind of wine.
Pasta, rice, and savory pies	Base your selection on the sauce or filling of the dish.
Rich food	Offer a dry wine.
Strong flavors	Offer a robust wine.

We would like to thank the chief oenologist of the renowned Frescobaldi Vineyard for his time and patience in explaining the history and progress of Tuscan wine (info@frescobaldi.it).

Conversione Metrica
METRIC CONVERSION

OVEN TEMPERATURES:

250°F	=	120°C	=	Gas Mark ½
275°F	=	140°C	=	Gas Mark 1
300°F	=	150°C	=	Gas Mark 2
325°F	=	160°C	=	Gas Mark 3
350°F	=	180°C	=	Gas Mark 4
375°F	=	190°C	=	Gas Mark 5
400°F	=	200°C	=	Gas Mark 6
425°F	=	220°C	=	Gas Mark 7
450°F	=	230°C	=	Gas Mark 8

GENERAL FORMULA:

Ounces to grams	Multiply ounces by 28.35
Pounds to grams	Multiply pounds by 453.5
Pounds to kilograms	Multiply pounds by .45
Cups (liquid) to liters	Multiply cups by .24

COMMON CONVERSIONS OF U.S. MEASUREMENTS TO METRIC:

½ ounce (dry weight)	=	14.17 grams
1 ounce (dry weight)	=	28.35 grams
1 cup (8 ounces, dry weight)	=	228 grams
1 cup (8 ounces, liquid)	=	236.6 milliliters
1 pound (16 ounces, dry)	=	454 grams
1 quart (32 ounces, liquid)	=	.95 liter

LENGTH CONVERSION:

1 inch	=	2.5 centimeters
8 inches	=	20.32 centimeters
10 inches	=	25.4 centimeters

Indice
INDEX

From Hippocrene's Regional Italian Cookbook Library

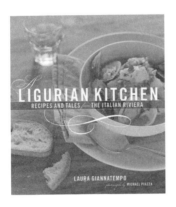

A LIGURIAN KITCHEN
Laura Giannatempo

Growing up, Laura Giannatempo spent most summers in Liguria, a narrow strip of beautiful coastal land in the northwest of Italy known as the Italian Riviera. Here she developed a passion for the region's food—refreshing and piquant, best known for its lavish use of fish, fresh herbs, and produce. The fifth in Hippocrene's regional Italian cookbook series, *A Ligurian Kitchen: Recipes and Tales from the Italian Riviera,* is a sophisticated love story between the author and the land whose foods and people she describes.

Original dishes like *Maltagliati con Pesto Piccantino* (Fresh Maltagliati with Spicy Purple Pesto) and *Ciuppin con Crostoni di Paprika* (Ligurian Seafood Bisque with Paprika Crostoni) are featured here, alongside such quintessential specialties as *Trofie con Pesto alla Genovese* (Trofie with Pesto, Green Beans, and Potatoes) and focaccia. One is tantalized by the delights of her Lavender *Panna Cotta* with Raspberry Puree, and tales of lovable uncles and an account of making pasta in the midst of a storm tempt just as much. Here is a zestful and spirited journey to Liguria, one that exemplifies "that extraordinary marriage of land and sea that is Ligurian cuisine." A vibrant account of people, food, and the place both find in our lives, in the best tradition of the cookbook memoir.

200 PAGES • 9 X 8 • 16 PAGE COLOR PHOTO INSERT • $29.00 HC
0-7818-1171-6 • (8)

CUCINA DI CALABRIA: TREASURED RECIPES AND FAMILY TRADITIONS FROM SOUTHERN ITALY
Mary Amabile Palmer

"[This volume] delivers fully on its promise of an authentic Southern Italian culinary experience."
—*Publishers Weekly*

For centuries Calabrian food has remained relatively undiscovered because few recipes were divulged outside of the region's tightly knit villages or even family circles. However, Mary Amabile Palmer has gathered a comprehensive collection of exciting, robust recipes from the home of her ancestors. *Cucina di Calabria* is a celebration of the cuisine she knows intimately and loves, a cuisine that is more adventurous and creative than that of most other parts of Italy. Nearly 200 recipes offer something for every cook, whether a novice or experienced. Anecdotes about Calabrian culture and history, traditions, festivals, folklore, and of course, the primary role that food plays in all aspects of Italian life complete this wonderful piece of culinary anthropology.
320 PAGES • 8 X 10 • $18.95 PB • 0-7818-1050-7 • (660)

CUCINA PIEMONTESE
Maria Grazia Asselle and Brian Yarvin

Cucina Piemontese provides an opportunity to explore Piedmont, known for its use of butter, cream, beef and truffles, as well as humbler ingredients such as pasta, polenta and root vegetables. More than 95 recipes have been rendered in this lovely volume, written with the American home cook in mind. Beginning with antipasti of *Cipolline in Agro Dolce* (Sweet-and-Sour Onions) or *Acciughe al Verde* (Anchovies in Green Sauce), journey though the region with *Tajarin con Sugo Burro e Salvia* (Egg Pasta with Butter and Sage Sauce) and *Brasato al Vino Rosso* (Beef Cooked in Red Wine), concluding with one of Piedmont's famous desserts, *Zuppa Inglese* (Ladyfinger Cake). A beautiful color insert, historical and cultural information, seasonal menus and a chapter on regional wines, including the famous Barolo, are all included in this insider's perspective into a fascinating cuisine.

159 PAGES • 6 X 9 •16 PAGE COLOR PHOTO INSERT • $27.50 HC
0-7818-1123-6 • (303)

SICILIAN FEASTS
Giovanna Bellia La Marca

Sicilian Feasts was born out of Giovanna La Marca's love for her native Sicily. She shares the history, customs, folklore, and the flavorful and varied cuisine of her beautiful Mediterranean island in these recipes, stories, and anecdotes. *Sicilian Feasts* offers more than 160 recipes, along with menus for holidays, notes on ingredients, list of suppliers, an introduction to the Sicilian language, and a glossary of food terms in Sicilian, Italian, and English.

Dishes such as *Mpanata*, a lamb pie from Ragusa, are sure to please one's most exacting guests. Simple methods and readily available ingredients allow even novices to create feasts in their kitchens. La Marca features examples of elaborate dishes created by the *monzu*, a class of eighteenth- and nineteenth-century professional cooks—ones you can now effortlessly recreate with modern appliances. She also introduces her readers to the practice of transforming almond paste into beautiful and realistic marzipan fruits, a traditional Sicilian art form. Illustrations demonstrate special techniques used to prepare these dishes in this delightful Italian cookbook.

240 PAGES • 6 X 9 • $24.95 HC (CAN $39.95)
0-7818-0967-3 • W • (539) • JUNE

CUISINES OF THE ALPS: RECIPES, DRINKS, AND LORE FROM FRANCE, SWITZERLAND, LIECHTENSTEIN, ITALY, GERMANY, AUSTRIA, AND SLOVENIA
Kay Shaw Nelson

A majestic mountain system of south-central Europe, forming about a 750-mile arc from the Gulf of Genoa in the Mediterranean Sea to Albania, the Alps have dozens of peaks taller than 10,000 feet. They are divided into the Western Alps (southeastern France, northwestern Italy), the Central Alps (north-central Italy, southern Switzerland, Liechtenstein), and the Eastern Alps (parts of Germany, Austria, and Slovenia), each of which contains several separate ranges.

In *All Along the Alps*, Kay Shaw Nelson offers more than 140 recipes that range from classic Italian pasta dishes to the wonderful fish preparations found in each of the regions. A section on beverages examines the wine production of these countries, from the well-known French and Italian wines to the more unfamiliar offerings of Slovenia and Liechtenstein, and an extensive historical and geographical introduction complements the comprehensive headnotes. The cuisine of the Alpine regions is ample evidence that the people who live there share a fondness for fine food, regardless of their regional or cultural differences.

220 PAGES • 6 X 9 • $24.95 HC • 0-7818-1058-2 • W • (59)

To Purchase Hippocrene Books

Contact your local bookstore, visit www.hippocrenebooks.com, call (718) 454-2366, or write to: HIPPOCRENE BOOKS, 171 Madison Avenue, New York, NY 10016. Please enclose check or money order, adding $5.00 shipping (UPS) for the first book, and $.50 for each additional book.
Prices subject to change without prior notice.